WINNING YOUR
JURY

The Psychology of Jury Selection and Decision-Making

WINNING YOUR
JURY

How to Litigate Like the Nation's
Top Trial Advocates

ROBERT G. KLEIN, ESQ.

DISCLAIMER

This publication is designed to provide accurate and authoritative information on the subject of jury selection and the litigation process primarily in the federal courts. The theories in this publication are based upon the author's experiences and based upon information accumulated over a substantial period of time. The reader should be mindful that predicting jury behavior is not an exact science and not all the theories set forth in this publication are accepted universally as the predictor of how a jury will decide any particular case.

Some of the information in this publication is based upon legal holdings, which can differ depending on the jurisdiction where the case was pending. This publication is sold with the understanding the publisher is not rendering legal, accounting, or other professional services. If legal advice or other expert assistance is required, the services of a competent professional person should be sought. It is important to confirm that the information has not been affected or changed by recent developments, traditional legal research developments or techniques.

TABLE OF CONTENTS

FOREWORD

"Law: The Epitome of The Art of Persuasion"

Prepare to be captivated by Robert Klein's electrifying exploration of the Jury's Mind in this groundbreaking masterpiece.

Right from the start, Klein conjures a spellbinding atmosphere, transforming the seemingly complex and dry Federal Rules of Civil Procedure into an enthralling journey that ignites curiosity and fuels the desire for victory.

Like a fearless explorer, Klein lays out a foolproof strategy, guiding us step-by-step towards the most favorable outcome. He reveals the hidden facets of law that elude most non-attorneys and even confound experienced lawyers. With a clear plan, he liberates litigators from the quagmire of the legal process, helping them comprehend the enigmatic mind of the Jury, where all decisions are made.

Whether you're a novice venturing into civil and criminal law or an expert in Intellectual Property, Klein breathes life into the crucial reasons we uphold the rule of law. It serves as a shield to safeguard individuals' lives, liberty, and pursuit of happiness, preventing years behind bars or drowning in crippling debt.

With a human touch and genuine sincerity, Klein takes us on a profound exploration of building the Theory of the Case, the art of Jury Selection, and the creative brilliance of Conjecture. He meticulously orchestrates every trial detail, from Opening to Closing Statements, leaving an indelible impression of sincerity, transparency, and humility that leaves no stone unturned in the minds of the Jury.

Attorney Klein ingeniously conveys the significance of the Theory of the Case while ensuring due diligence. He seamlessly integrates evolving legal principles with his Theory, relentlessly pursuing truth as the guiding force towards the best possible outcomes. His work is a lifeline for those wrongfully accused, facing imprisonment for crimes they didn't commit, or small business owners locked in intellectual property battles against deep-pocketed corporations armed with ruthless legal teams. Klein empowers them to defend themselves against every deceitful tactic, every hidden rule, allowing them to secure lasting freedom.

As a non-attorney with 24 cases in the United States Trademark Trial and Appeals Board, the TTAB, I held my own for 14 years. However, when faced with an Intellectual Property dispute over trademarks, I found myself out of my depth. We engaged a local attorney who failed to heed Klein's advice on due diligence, leaving us adrift, facing exorbitant attorney fees of up to $1,000,000.

Lost and desperate, I turned to the internet and discovered Robert. Generously, he shared his book with me. Now armed with the knowledge to decipher and unveil all the hidden aspects my attorney never disclosed, I've taken charge, guiding my attorney on how to win the case. Law school fails to impart the invaluable insights that Robert Klein masterfully unveils in his book. It teaches us how to think, not just push papers.

This book not only imparts eye-opening wisdom but also unveils the rich tapestry of case law that underpins our legal system. It transforms legal enthusiasts into legal prodigies, democratizing the world of law for all truth-seekers, champions of justice, aspiring lawyers, and those forced into the legal arena by circumstances beyond their control. No longer will the law remain the exclusive domain of the privileged few who can afford astronomical hourly rates.

Let us dismantle the barriers, release the law from its ivory tower, and make it accessible to all who crave knowledge, need protection, or yearn to unravel the mysteries of this nation's foundation. Let us foster a deeper appreciation for truth-seekers, justice warriors, and ensure that no one falls victim to the schemes of the unscrupulous who exploit the innocent in their quest for power and wealth.

May this review open your eyes to the astonishing world of law and the pursuit of truth that Robert Klein so magnanimously bestows. His work is a breath of fresh air, brimming with honesty, sincerity, and the humble curiosity of a student, yet backed by the wisdom of a professor. Klein's realistic approach simplifies law, making it accessible to all, while cautioning against those lawyers who abuse their power. This is a groundbreaking masterpiece that lays the foundation for a more enlightened world, where common sense and the potent weapon of law combine to forge a civilized society.

This book is a revelation. Brace yourself for an extraordinary journey.

God bless you, and God bless America!

– Matt Fogarty, MD

INTRODUCTION
HOW JURIES DECIDE CASES

Several years ago, I was the lead trial attorney on a jury trial that lasted five months. My client was a building contractor who worked mostly installing low voltage systems for public entities.

I was defending against claims brought by 36 former employees of my client who claim they were underpaid for what is known as the state mandated prevailing wage on public works construction projects. This is what is called a wage and hour case and includes claims these employees were improperly classified. The prevailing wage law requires employers to pay a certain wage based upon the kind of work the employee is performing. The classification of someone who performs labor by digging trenches gets paid a different rate from someone classified as an electrician working with high voltage.

The jury pool was primarily blue collar with a high concentration of Hispanic and people from eastern European countries. Based upon our trial estimate it took the court eight weeks to screen prospective jurors just to get enough people to sit on a jury for five months. You would think that most of the people that were sent up to our department for the trial would have retired because it would seem retired people have the time to sit for a trial of that length, but that was not the case. We got several people who were government employees or worked for a civil minded company that agreed to pay their salaries for this lengthy trial.

The trial was grueling. One of the plaintiffs was residing in Russia and another was in Guatemala. The plaintiffs used some technology where these witnesses in remote locations could be questioned about the case. The jury, the court, and the lawyers could actually watch and interact with these witnesses in real time. It was even possible to put a document in a facsimile-like machine and have the document appear in seconds in a remote country, making it possible to question these witnesses about a document as if they were sitting in the courtroom. Another juror, who was the leader of the plaintiffs, was a convicted felon having been convicted for burglary of construction tools from his former employer. Dealing with a convicted party in a civil case is also challenging.

Throughout the trial the judge gave us anonymous notes from one juror who was showing a strong bias toward the plaintiffs and disdain toward the lawyers for the defense. Because of the length of this trial the judge ruled, over objection by the defense, that the plaintiffs' testimony could be supplied by declarations prepared by their attorney.

Any defendant that wanted to cross examine a party was given that opportunity. That did not seem to make a difference because most of the plaintiffs did not seem to have any knowledge of the events giving rise to their claims and had little or no knowledge about the prevailing wage laws.

The deliberations took a month. When the jury finally reached their verdict, it turned out we won over 55% of the claims. On the claims we lost the plaintiffs were awarded about 25% of their settlement demands. When you get a verdict like that the lawyers for the defense claim victory while their clients feel they suffered a defeat.

After this experience I was obsessed with understanding how juries decide cases. Under the California Constitution in order to reach a verdict in a civil trial there must be at least 3/4 of the jurors agreeing on the decision. If the jury foreperson cannot get at least nine out of twelve to agree on a verdict the court can declare a mistrial.

Our decision was 10-2 with the two voting for our side were Caucasian middle-class women and the other ten were Hispanic; eight of which were women and two of those eight were middle class with the balance were perceived by me to be blue collar individuals.

After the trial our opposing counsel, who practiced primarily in conservative Orange County, confessed that if this case were tried in Orange County with a conservative and primarily Caucasian jury pool the decision would have been 10-2 in favor of the defense.

I realized that juries do not decide cases based upon the facts or the law. If they did then every verdict would be unanimous. How is it that 12 people hearing the same facts and are provided with the same law come to different conclusions? Why does the California Constitution require only 9 of 12 to agree on the verdict?

The United States Supreme court has some of the smartest and most experienced lawyers and jurists yet many of their decision are 5-4, 6-3, or 7-2. We hear repeatedly that the make-up of the Supreme Court is composed of 6 conservatives and 3 liberals and how that composition can change the social structure of our country for years to come. Based upon that political make-up of the Supreme Court we get shifts in rulings on topics like abortion, gun control, immigration and entitlements to social security or Medicare.

I spent months researching the subject of how jurors decide cases by reading books on jury selection and listening to tapes from some of the country's top trial lawyers, judges, and legal scholars. Here is what I found.

CHAPTER 1

WHAT MAKES A GOOD TRIAL LAWYER

When I was starting out as an attorney after passing the bar, I became obsessed with trying to figure out how it is that some trial lawyers continuously get large jury verdicts. What makes a good trial lawyer? I started reading everything I could find on the subject. I listened to tapes, and I attended seminars. One lecturer, who I found immensely helpful, was a fellow named Irving Younger. He was much acclaimed as a lawyer, a professor, a judge, and a scholar and he had some very entertaining tapes that ran for hours on all different topics of trial advocacy. What I learned from Judge Younger's tapes was through an interesting story he told about when he was growing up in New York during the 1940s.

During the summer months, every day that the Yankees were in town, his parents gave him money to get on a streetcar, buy a ticket, eat a hotdog, and watch the Yankees play baseball.

In the 1940s, the Yankees had a terrific team, and their star center fielder was Joe DiMaggio. Irving Younger, as a young boy, watched Joe DiMaggio play over 1000 times. His first job out-of-college many years later was as a cub reporter for the New York Giants. In the New York Giants' center field, there was a fellow named Willie Mays. And he watched Willie Mays play many times, as well.

After many of the games where Willie Mays was playing centerfield, Irving Younger went to the newsroom and spoke enthusiastically with the more experienced and seasoned sports writers about what he saw Wille Mays do. He would say, "You would not belief what Willie did today. The ball was hit to center field. Willie started running and turned himself into a human doughnut rolling toward the center field wall. He then raised his glove and made the catch. He must be the greatest centerfielder who ever played the game." He was surprised to hear the other reporters said: "Willie's good no doubt about it, but the greatest centerfielder to ever play the game was Joe DiMaggio." In response Younger said: "You've got to be kidding. I've seen Joe DiMaggio play a thousand times, and not once did Joe DiMaggio make a play that Willie Mays makes three times in every game."

The more he thought about it he agreed. When the ball was hit to center field there was Joe DiMaggio pounding his glove, the ball would fall into his glove, and he would toss the ball back into the infield and the game would resume. The reason his elders felt that way is because DiMaggio was reliable; he was dependable. You could trust Joe DiMaggio that if the ball were hit in his direction, he would catch it. When it came to Willie Mays, he was exciting, but you never knew whether or not Willie was going to catch the ball.

The lesson of the story is that a good trial lawyer is someone who is reliable, dependable and credible. It is a lawyer who comes into the courtroom prepared, dressed appropriately, and organized. The counsel table in front of him is neatly established. He has his files and folders, and he can find everything within a few seconds. It is key to establish credibility with the jury for being dependable and reliable.

Credibility is related to the Greek concept of ethos, pathos, and logos. Ethos refers to ethics. The main thing you need to do when starting a case as a trial lawyer is to create that ethos with the jury. One way of doing it is, instead of being an advocate, be more like a teacher.

Do not overstate your case to the jury. You want to come off as being in control and reliable. You are not going to overstate or argue things that you cannot necessarily prove. Instead, try to convert your role to more of a teacher, who explains the story in a very compassionate, non-confrontational way. That is how you establish credibility with the jury.

CHAPTER 2

DECIDING TO TAKE THE CASE

When a new client comes into your office and tells you about the kind of case that he has, before you even really listen to the facts of the case, you need to run a conflicts check. This is when you see who all the parties of the case are, and you determine whether you have a conflict of interest. For example, whether you have a preexisting relationship with any of the parties or whether you have some kind of financial interest in the outcome of the case. It is particularly important to establish a conflict check early on because if you do not do it, you can find yourself being disqualified down the line.

One of the things you want to consider is if you are being asked to represent either two plaintiffs or two defendants. You must determine whether there is a conflict between representing either two plaintiffs or two defendants. Even though the two parties may have similar claims or defenses in the case, they might have claims against each other for indemnification, which would create a conflict.

First, you must identify whether there exists a conflict and if there is a conflict, consider whether you can resolve the conflict by having full disclosure and a written waiver of conflict of interest signed by the clients.

In the first interview, your client is going to tell you what this case is about. Before you even decide to take the case, you are going to want to engage in interviews with some key players and maybe review some of the key documents, so you can get a feel for the validity of the case. You also need to explain to your client the costs that are going to be involved. You do not want to misrepresent or understate the value of the case and you do not want to overstate the chances of succeeding.

Only take cases when your client is an honest person, and their case has validity. It is not always easy in your initial interview to tell if the person asking you to represent them is an honest person, but there are several signs. Listen carefully and watch their body language when they are telling you about the events that led to this lawsuit. Honest people tend to behave consistently and in a predictable manner. They do not often change their stories or offer conflicting information.

Try to be sensitive if they are not being transparent about their intentions, actions, and motives. They should not be afraid to share information and are comfortable discussing their thoughts and feelings.

If they are a defendant and are being sued for fraud with serious allegations being made against them, listen carefully to their explanations. If they spend too much time and use too many words to try to convince you the allegations are false be skeptical. If a person is being truthful their explanation does not need to involve a long and involved story.

A UCLA professor and researcher in the field of psychology produced a theory on communication called the 7-38-55 theory. Under this theory, 7% of communication is based on words, 38% is based upon the tone of voice, and 55% is body language. On a study of the components of lying, a Harvard Business school professor found that on average, liars use more words than truth tellers and use far more third- person pronouns. They start talking about others with vague pronouns in order put distance between themselves and the lie.[1]

Non-verbal cues, such as facial expressions, body language, and tone of voice, can provide insight into a person's emotional state and level of comfort with what they are saying.

Be cynical if you are the third or fourth attorney that was interviewed by this new client. People looking to hire an attorney in a litigation matter will keep interviewing attorneys until they find one that will tell them what they want to hear. A prospective client recently interviewed me about setting aside a $4 million default judgment.

I felt I could set aside the default judgment but told her if the case went before a judge or jury it was likely there would still be a judgment against her. The strategy was to set aside the default and then try to negotiate a lesser judgment.

If it could not be negotiated downward, then we could raise some defenses to reduce the amount of a judgment at trial. This prospective client interviewed 10 other lawyers. The first nine told her what I said, but the last attorney told her she could walk away without owing any money. She hired him.

Before agreeing to take a case, you must consider the legal merits of the case, meaning whether your assessment is the case has a good chance of succeeding in court. Review the facts and evidence

---

[1] Chris Voss *Never Split the Difference*

to determine whether there is a legal basis for the case and whether there are any potential legal defenses that may be raised.

Consider the potential client's personality, goals, and expectations. You will want to make sure you can work effectively with the client and that the client's goals are aligned with your strategy.

Lawsuits are timely and expensive. You need to assess the amount of time and resources required to handle the case effectively and whether your client understands the costs and fees involved. This requires you to consider the complexity of the case, the number of parties involved, and the potential costs of pursuing the case.

Before you agree to represent a client in a litigation matter review documents and discuss the facts with people who witnessed the events but do not have an interest in the outcome. If you represent a client who is not an honest person or has a meritless case it will only create a conflict between you and this client as the case progresses.

CHAPTER 3

DEVELOPING THE THEORY OF THE CASE

In litigation, a theory of the case, a theme, and a tagline are all important elements that help shape and communicate the core arguments and narrative of a legal case. While they are interconnected, they serve different purposes and are used at various stages of the litigation process.

■ THEORY OF THE CASE

A theory of the case refers to the overarching legal strategy or framework that guides the presentation of evidence and arguments to support a party's position in a lawsuit. It provides a coherent and logical explanation of what happened and why the party should prevail. A theory of the case typically incorporates the relevant facts, applicable laws, and supporting evidence to construct a persuasive narrative that supports the party's desired outcome. It serves as a roadmap for the legal team to organize and present their case in a cohesive manner.

Developing a theory of the case involves a thorough analysis of the evidence, legal principles, and the client's objectives. It requires identifying the key issues, strengths, and weaknesses of the case, as well as anticipating the opposing party's arguments. The theory of the case serves as a foundation for all subsequent litigation strategies, including case preparation, witness examination, expert testimony, and legal arguments presented to the court or jury.

■ THEME

A theme is a central idea or persuasive concept that underlies the theory of the case. It is a powerful storytelling tool that helps the legal team communicate their theory to the judge, jury, or opposing counsel in a compelling and memorable way. A theme is usually presented as a concise and emotionally resonant statement that encapsulates the essence of the case and resonates with the factfinder.

The theme aims to evoke an emotional response, create empathy, and make complex legal issues more relatable and understandable to the factfinder. It often reflects the core narrative of the case and highlights the party's position and desired outcome. For example, in a personal injury case, a theme might be "Justice for the Injured" to emphasize the harm suffered by the plaintiff and the need for compensation.

■ TAGLINE

A tagline, in the context of litigation, refers to a short, memorable phrase or slogan that encapsulates the essence of the case or summarizes the party's position. It is a concise and impactful statement that can be used in trial advocacy, media coverage, or other forms of communication to distill the main message of the case into a few words.

Unlike a theory of the case or a theme, a tagline is often used for marketing and public relations purposes to create a memorable impression in the minds of the audience. It is designed to capture attention, generate interest, and simplify complex legal concepts. Taglines are commonly used in high-profile cases or to create a public perception surrounding a legal matter. For example, the tagline "Fighting for Truth and Freedom" could be used to rally public support in a high-stakes constitutional case.

To summarize a theory of the case is the overarching legal strategy that guides a party's arguments and evidence. The theme is a central idea that underlies the theory and helps create a persuasive narrative. A tagline, on the other hand, is a concise and memorable statement that summarizes the case's essence and can be used for marketing and public relations purposes. Together, these elements contribute to shaping the persuasive communication and presentation of a legal case.

■ DEVELOPING YOUR THEORY OF THE CASE

Before you even file your initial pleadings, whether a complaint, cross complaint or answer you need to develop your initial theory of the case. I say your initial theory of the case because your theory of the case can change as you gather additional facts during the discovery process. What you are trying to do early in the litigation is develop your discovery plan and your theory of the case.

The first step in litigation, and in eventually choosing an ideal juror for your case is by establishing your theory of the case. This must be done early in the litigation. A theory of a case could be simply a couple of sentences or short paragraphs of what you would tell the jury about your case and why you should prevail. In order to prove your theory of the case, you have to develop a discovery plan to prove all these points with evidence.

A lawyer's theory of the case refers to the argument or strategy that a lawyer will use to convince a judge or jury to find in favor of their client. It is the central narrative that ties together all of the evidence, testimony, and legal arguments presented by the lawyer throughout the trial and litigation.

A theory of the case is not just a simple statement of what the case is about, but rather a carefully constructed and persuasive explanation of how the facts and legal principles apply to support the client's position. It considers the strengths and weaknesses of the case, as well as the potential biases and perspectives of the judge or jury. A cogent theory of the case is essential to provide focus on each aspect of the litigation starting with drafting the pleadings, conducting written discovery, taking depositions to conducting voir dire in jury selection, selecting jurors, examination of witness through closing argument.

Developing a strong theory of the case is a crucial part of trial preparation for lawyers, as it guides their approach to presenting evidence, cross-examining witnesses, and making legal arguments. It is a dynamic process that can evolve as new information or evidence emerges during the trial, but the central narrative of the theory remains consistent and focused on achieving the best possible outcome for the client. The best theories of the case are those that reflect ordinary life experiences. The goal of a jury trial is persuasion. The best way to persuade is by presenting a theory of a case to which most people can relate.

Assuming you are trying a case against a financial advisor who is accused of "churning" your client's stock portfolio to generate commissions. Churning stock portfolios is a type of securities fraud that involves a broker engaging in excessive trading of a customer's account for the purpose of generating commissions. The theory of the case in a churning case would be that the broker breached their fiduciary duty to the customer by excessively trading the account for their own financial gain. You want your prospective juror to relate emotionally with the experience of your client by conjuring up their past memories and emotions from their experience in a similar situation. This information can be revealed during voir dire.

Your theory of the case must be factually correct and cannot be attacked as untrustworthy. This requires establishing facts that are not subject to change. To find facts that are not subject to change means locating facts in the form of documents, photographs, physical evidence, tape recordings or any fact fixed to a medium that will withstand an attack if the evidence lacks authentication or foundation. Facts beyond change are facts that will be believed by the jury despite attempts by the opposing side to dispute or modify them.

CHAPTER 4

CREATING A TAGLINE

As part of the theory of the case, you want to develop a certain theme and a tagline that you can use to trigger certain responses from a jury. The theory of the case is a couple of sentences or a referred paragraph that explains why you believe your client should prevail. The tagline can be a word or a short phrase. After you develop the theory of the case, you need to create a tagline based upon a theme. The tagline needs to be refined before you start trial, but it is a good idea to create your initial tagline before you engage in discovery. A tagline is based upon a triggering event in a lawsuit. For example, in just about every lawsuit involving a business dispute, there is a certain relationship that is established between the parties.

They may be partners in a business, a majority shareholder to a minority shareholder, a stockbroker to an investor or any similar relationship engaged in for a commercial purpose. Whatever it is, there is a certain expectation that this relationship is going to be beneficial to the parties. At some time during the course of the relationship, one party did something that shocked the other party which invoked the response, "That S.O.B," making them think the other party in this relationship is an untrustworthy crook, which resulted in the filing of a lawsuit. This betrayal is the triggering event. Once you have identified the triggering event you can create an effective tagline or short phrase that identifies the essence of the dispute in the litigation that is based upon that triggering event.

The tagline is a memorable phrase that summarizes the main argument and anchors the theory of the case.

The tagline in jury persuasion generally refers to a brief and memorable phrase that summarizes the main argument or theme of a lawyer's case in a trial. The purpose of a tagline is to capture the attention of the jury, help them remember key points, and persuade them to find in favor of the lawyer's client.

Examples of a tagline used for jury persuasion might be: "Nobody is above the law," "No good deed goes unpunished," "It was just business," "A chain is only as strong as its weakest link" in a product liability case, or "Truth Prevails" in a fraud trial, or "When it would benefit him, he has lied" to show the party is a con man and liar. The tagline should be simple, powerful, and easily understandable by the jury, while also resonating with their values and beliefs.

In one case, a nanny taking care of a young baby who had Colic shook the baby and caused brain damage. The triggering event was when the nanny shook the baby. The theory of the case was clear; the nanny was negligent, but its tagline was: "This didn't have to happen." Once you continue to repeat that tagline throughout the litigation including during voir dire, opening statement, cross examination, and closing argument, the jury starts remembering the tagline and they associate your case and the theory of your case with that tagline.

We all remember Martin Luther King's famous "I had a dream" speech. In that speech Dr. King kept repeating the phase "I had a dream." While you may not remember what specifically he said following that line, just hearing the phrase "I had a dream" was enough to remind us about the struggles against racial discrimination.

■ BREAKING DOWN THE THEORY OF THE CASE INTO PHRASES

Theme lines can be sentences, phrases, or just a word that is a shorthand way to state a theme and essence of the case that may not capture the entire theory of the case.

Sometimes you will need to create more than one phrase or tagline. The term "phrase" and "tagline" are often used interchangeably depending on their length. Often you can develop a theme phrase from a position your opposition took in the litigation. In a complex trademark infringement case, the defense theory may be that the first sale doctrine was a defense to a trademark infringement claim.

The CEO of the software company testified at his deposition that his company merely purchased genuine goods and resold those goods without any change. He also testified that very few of his potential customers who tried the software ever ended up purchasing or licensing the software. Therefore, there were no profits or provable damages. One theme phrase or tag line could then be "No deception, no confusion, no harm." Another tag line could be "Those who tried it didn't buy it."

In the O. J Simpson murder trial, after the prosecution had O. J. Simpson try on a pair of blood-soaked gloves that did not fit, famed trial lawyer Johnny Cochran created the phrase: "If it doesn't fit, you must acquit." That summed up the essence of a lengthy trial with that phrase becoming the single most identifiable part of the trial. The incident that spawned that brilliant tagline phrase was the turning point in the trial leading to acquittal.

If you are litigating a fraud case and you learn from your investigator the defendant has been sued repeatedly for fraud or has been convicted of a crime for dishonesty and you want to stress those facts to the jury that he is not trustworthy, your theme phrase may be "When it would benefit him, he has lied."

■ USING A TAGLINE TO PERSUADE JURORS

A well-crafted tagline can help to simplify complex legal arguments and make them more accessible to jurors. It can also help to create an emotional connection with jurors and reinforce the key points that the lawyer wants to make. A plaintiff's lawyer in a medical malpractice case might use the tagline to appeal to the jurors' sense of justice and responsibility. Similarly, a defense lawyer in a product liability case might use the tagline to appeal to the jurors' sense of fairness and the presumption of innocence.

CHAPTER 5

DRAFTING THE PLEADINGS

■ IDENTIFY THE LEGAL THEORY

You've met with your new client and heard the reasons why he or she thinks they have a case. Sometimes it is clear the legal theories that are involved. If your client was involved in a car accident the legal theories are relatively straight forward, however sometimes it is not always clear all the legal claims that are involved in your client's case. This is where you need to conduct research.

Lawyers normally start their research by going to their on-line legal research guides. There are several different companies that offer comprehensive research tools including access to cases and statutes for all the states in the country and for the federal system. They also offer a variety of legal treatises and practice guides. The first place to look would be in the practice guides and treatises.

Chances are you will know the general area of law involved. If the controversy involves a dispute over real estate, you find a treatise or practice guide on real property law. These practice guides provide a detailed analysis of all aspects of the law in that area.

One day I got a call from a client who received a phone call from somebody who said he bought my client's house and wanted to know when my client and his family were going to vacate the premises. My client was shocked to hear about this sale and was understandably upset since he knew nothing about this sale.

I learned that years earlier he had temporarily placed this property in a trust for his ex-girlfriend to facilitate a loan. His ex-girlfriend never transferred the title back to my client. Years later she sold this property to this investor for a fraction of the value and pocketed the sales proceeds.

In drafting the lawsuit my goal was to state all possible causes of action my client had against his ex-girlfriend, the person who bought the property who was not what is called a BFP (bona fide purchaser for value), and the real estate agents involved.

When I drafted the complaint for the lawsuit that followed, I included claims for: Cancellation of Deed, Declaratory Relief, Quiet Title, Breach of Fiduciary Duty, Constructive Fraud, Civil Conspiracy, Imposition of a Constructive Trust, Breach of Contract, Promissory Estoppel, and Negligence.

■ JURY INSTRUCTIONS GIVE YOU THE ROAD MAP

After identifying all the legal theories, you next look over the jury instructions for the elements you need to plead and prove to prevail on each legal cause of action. Jury instructions are extremely important in understanding the issues in a lawsuit, as they provide guidance to the jury on how to interpret and apply the law to the facts of the case. Jury instructions are typically given by the judge to the jury before they begin deliberating, and they explain the legal standards that the jury must use to make their decision.

By reviewing the jury instructions early in the case, you can gain a clearer understanding of the legal issues involved in a lawsuit, including the elements of the claims or defenses being asserted, the burden of proof, and the legal principles that apply. This understanding can be particularly important for parties to a lawsuit, as it can help them to evaluate the strengths and weaknesses of their case, and to identify any potential grounds for appeal.

To show other important uses of jury instruction, I had a client who was being sued in the ninth circuit for trademark infringement under the Lanham Act. The allegations were that he was selling counterfeit goods, a profoundly serious accusation.

The federal court system in our country is organized into 12 regional circuits, each of which is overseen by a federal court of appeals. The federal district courts are the trial courts of the federal court system and are responsible for hearing both civil and criminal cases that arise under federal law. I practice in California which is the ninth circuit. The Ninth Circuit Court of Appeals is one of the 12 regional circuits of the federal court system in the United States including California.

The ninth circuit model jury instruction will tell you everything you need to know when you are representing a party in a trademark infringement case or in any case filed in the federal court. It will list all the various claims that can be raised under the Lanham Act, the elements of each claim that the plaintiff needs to prove and all the available affirmative defenses.

Here is an example of the ninth circuit jury instruction:

15.20 Derivative Liability—Inducing Infringement:
"A person is liable for trademark infringement by another if the person intentionally induced another to infringe the trademark. The plaintiff has the burden of proving each of the following by a preponderance of the evidence:

1. [Name of direct infringer] infringed the plaintiff's trademark.
2. The defendant intentionally induced [name of direct infringer] to infringe plaintiff's trademark; and
3. The plaintiff was damaged by the infringement.

If you find that each of the elements on which the plaintiff has the burden of proof has been proved, your verdict should be for the plaintiff. If, on the other hand, the plaintiff has failed to prove any of these elements, your verdict should be for the defendant."

What is particularly helpful when reviewing the jury instructions is the "comments" section which explains the legal authority for the specific rule of law. For example, the model rule 15.20 is titled-Derivative Liability-Inducing infringement. The comment section after citing the instruction reads:

"Regarding liability for inducing another to infringe a trademark, see Inwood Labs. Inc. v. Ives Labs. Inc., 456 U.S. 844, 853-54 (1982) ("[I]f a manufacturer or distributor intentionally induces another to infringe a trademark, or if it continues to supply its product to one whom it knows or has reason to know is engaging in trademark infringement, the manufacturer is contributorily responsible for any harm done as a result of the deceit [by the direct infringer].").

See also Lockheed Martin Corp. v. Network Sols., Inc., 194 F.3d 980, 983-84 (9th Cir. 1999) (noting that one branch of contributory infringement occurs when defendant "intentionally induces a third party to infringe the plaintiff's mark"). Reviewing the jury instructions can not only help you prepare your pleading and your case outline, but it is also a terrific source of legal authority you can use when you draft motions and legal briefs.

■ THE COMPLAINT

When drafting the complaint your goal is to state a viable claim or cause of action to avoid a challenge to your complaint by a demurrer in state court or a motion to dismiss for failing to state a claim in federal court.

Drafting pleadings for a lawsuit can be a complex and time-consuming process, and it's important to ensure that the documents are accurate, comprehensive, and comply with all legal requirements. Here are some general steps to follow when drafting pleadings for a lawsuit:

Begin by identifying the plaintiff(s) and defendant(s) and clearly stating their names and roles in the case and clearly state the claims being made by the plaintiff(s) against the defendant(s). This may include allegations of breach of contract, negligence, or other legal violations. This takes legal research including a review of jury instructions that define the law at this early stage of the litigation. By reviewing jury instructions at this phase, you will know each element you will have to plead and prove.

Make sure to provide a detailed factual background to support the claims being made, including dates, times, locations, and any other relevant information. And state what the plaintiff(s) are seeking as relief from the defendant(s). This may include monetary damages, injunctive relief, or other remedies.

Review the local court rules and make sure your pleading complies with all relevant legal requirements, such as formatting, jurisdictional requirements, and statute of limitations. After drafting the initial pleadings, review them carefully for accuracy, clarity, and completeness. Make any necessary revisions before filing them with the court.

■ ANSWER, CROSS COMPLAINT, COUNTERCLAIM

The pleadings in the case consisting of the complaint, the answer or any cross complaint frame the issues for the lawsuit by identifying the relevant issue in dispute. This sets the parameters for the discovery and for motions that follow.

A cross-complaint or counterclaim is a legal document filed by a defendant in response to a plaintiff's complaint in a civil lawsuit. The purpose of a cross- complaint or counterclaim is to assert claims against the plaintiff that arise out of the same transaction or occurrence that is the subject of the plaintiff's complaint.

A cross-complaint is filed by a defendant against a co-defendant or third-party defendant, while a counter-claim is filed against the original plaintiff who filed the complaint. Both types of pleadings are used to assert claims for relief against another party in the same lawsuit.

For example, if a plaintiff sues a defendant for breach of contract, the defendant may file a counterclaim for breach of contract against the plaintiff. Alternatively, if two defendants are sued by a plaintiff, one defendant may file a cross-complaint against the other defendant for indemnity or contribution.

A cross-complaint or counterclaim allows the defendant to assert claims against the plaintiff or other defendants that may otherwise be time-barred or waive their right to bring the claim. It can also help to streamline the litigation process by allowing all claims arising out of the same transaction or occurrence to be resolved in a single lawsuit.

■ AFFIRMATIVE DEFENSES WHEN DRAFTING THE ANSWER

When representing a defendant, you will need to plead and prove all available affirmative defenses. An affirmative defense is a defense raised by the defendant in a legal case, in which the defendant admits to committing the acts that are alleged by the plaintiff but seeks to avoid liability by asserting additional facts.

A waiver is a legal term that refers to the voluntary relinquishment or abandonment of a known legal right or privilege. In the context of an affirmative defense, a waiver occurs when the defendant fails to raise an affirmative defense in a timely manner, thereby waiving their right to assert that defense later in the case.

If a defendant fails to raise an affirmative defense in a timely manner, they may be deemed to have waived that defense. This means that they will be precluded from raising that defense later in the case. If you are defending a lawsuit one of the most important things to do is make sure you have alleged all your affirmative defenses in your answer.

Fed. Rule Civ. Proc. Rule 8 describes the general rules of pleading in the federal courts and states that a claim for Relief must contain:

1. A short and plain statement of the grounds for the court's jurisdiction unless the court already has jurisdiction and the claim for relief needs no new Denials—Responding to the Substance. A denial must fairly respond to the substance of the allegation.
2. General and Specific Denials. A party that intends in good faith to deny all the allegations of a pleading—including the jurisdictional grounds—may do so by a general denial. A party that does not intend to deny all the allegations must

either specifically deny designated allegations or generally deny all except those specifically admitted.

3. Denying Part of an Allegation. A party that intends in good faith to deny only part of an allegation must admit the part that is true and deny the rest.

4. Lacking Knowledge or Information. A party that lacks knowledge or information sufficient to form a belief about the truth of an allegation must so state, and the statement has the effect of a denial.

5. Effect of Failing to Deny. An allegation—other than one relating to the amount of damages—is admitted if a responsive pleading is required and the allegation is not denied. If a responsive pleading is not required, an allegation is considered denied or avoided.

Affirmative Defenses

In responding to a pleading, a party must affirmatively state any avoidance or affirmative defense, including:

- accord and satisfaction
- arbitration and award
- assumption of risk. contributory negligence
- duress
- estoppel
- failure of consideration
- fraud
- illegality
- injury by fellow servant. laches
- license
- payment

- release
- res judicata
- statute of frauds
- statute of limitations
- and waiver.

■ THE DEMURRER AND MOTION TO DISMISS

A demurrer is a legal document used in state court civil cases that challenges the legal sufficiency of a plaintiff's complaint. It is also sometimes referred to as a motion to dismiss for failure to state a claim. The purpose of a demurrer is to assert that even if the plaintiff's allegations in the complaint are true, they do not state a valid legal claim against the defendant.

When a defendant files a demurrer, the court reviews the plaintiff's complaint and the arguments presented in the demurrer and determines whether the complaint is legally sufficient to proceed with the case. If the court finds that the complaint fails to state a claim, it may grant the demurrer and dismiss the case. More commonly the court gives leave to amend which gives the plaintiff more chances to state a legally viable claim.

Courts generally have discretion in granting or denying leave to amend a complaint. However, there are some circumstances where a court may deny leave to amend a complaint. The courts consider if the proposed amendment would not cure the defects in the original complaint or would be futile, the court may deny leave to amend.

If allowing an amendment would unfairly prejudice the opposing party, the court may deny leave to amend. For example, if the opposing party has already expended significant time and resources in responding to the original complaint, allowing an amendment may cause undue hardship or delay.

If the plaintiff has unreasonably delayed in seeking to amend the complaint, the court may deny leave to amend. This can occur when the plaintiff had ample opportunity to raise the new claims or allegations in the original complaint but failed to do so. And if the proposed amendment is made in bad faith or for an improper purpose, such as to harass the opposing party or to needlessly prolong the litigation or if the amendment would violate filing deadlines established by the court or by statute the court may deny leave to amend.

In general, courts will allow a party to amend a complaint if it will promote the fair and efficient resolution of the case. However, if the proposed amendment would unduly prejudice the opposing party, delay the proceedings, or be futile, the court may deny leave to amend.

The role of a demurrer in state court is to allow defendants to challenge the legal sufficiency of a plaintiff's complaint early in the litigation process. By doing so, the demurrer can potentially save both parties time and resources by resolving a case before it proceeds to discovery or trial.

It's important to note that demurrers are not appropriate in every case and may not be granted in situations where the complaint contains enough factual allegations to support a claim, even if the legal theory is flawed.

The counterpart to a demurrer in state court is a motion to dismiss in federal court. A motion to dismiss in federal court civil cases under Rule 12 also requests the court dismiss a plaintiff's complaint before trial. A motion to dismiss can be filed at any time during the litigation process, but it is most commonly filed at the beginning of a case before the parties engage in discovery or trial. It is often used as a tool to dismiss cases that are unlikely to succeed or to narrow the scope of the issues that will be litigated in the case.

Dispositive Motions

Once the issues are established by the pleadings, other motions can be filed that further challenge the existence of the lawsuit including a motion for judgment on the pleadings or a motion for summary judgment.

■ JUDGMENT ON THE PLEADINGS

Judgment on the pleadings is a legal procedure that can be used to resolve a case in a civil lawsuit without a trial. It occurs when one party in the case files a motion for judgment on the pleadings, arguing that the facts alleged in the pleadings of the other party are not in dispute and that the law supports a judgment in their favor.

To obtain a judgment on the pleadings, the moving party must convince the court that there are no material facts in dispute, and that the legal issues can be decided based solely on the pleadings (i.e., the complaint, answer, and any other relevant pleadings filed by the parties).

If the court agrees with the moving party and finds that the facts alleged in the pleadings are not in dispute and that the law supports a judgment in their favor, it will grant the motion for judgment on the pleadings and issue a final judgment in the case.

It's important to note that a judgment on the pleadings is only appropriate when there are no material facts in dispute, and the moving party can show that the case can be resolved on the pleadings alone. If there are material facts in dispute or if there is a need for additional evidence, the case may need to proceed to trial. The court only considers the pleading and any matter to which the court can take judicial notice in ruling on a motion for judgment on the pleadings.

■ SUMMARY JUDGMENT

Summary judgment is a legal procedure in the form of a motion made to the court that can be used to resolve a case in a civil lawsuit without a trial. It occurs when one party in the case files a motion for summary judgment, arguing that there are no genuine issues of material fact and that they are entitled to judgment as a matter of law.

To obtain a summary judgment, the moving party must convince the court that there are no material facts in dispute and that the legal issues can be decided based on the evidence presented in the case. The moving party must also show that they are entitled to judgment as a matter of law, meaning that even if all the disputed facts were resolved in favor of the other party, the moving party would still win.

Summary judgment is often used when the facts of the case are not in dispute and the only question is how the law applies to those facts. It can also be used to narrow the issues to be resolved at trial, or to dispose of a case altogether.

If there are genuine issues of material fact or if there is a need for additional evidence, the case may need to proceed to trial.

In ruling on a motion for summary judgment, the court considers the evidence presented by the parties in the form of affidavits, declarations, deposition transcripts, and other documents, as well as any admissions made during the discovery process.

The evidence must be admissible and must be based on personal knowledge or other reliable sources. The court will not consider hearsay or speculation and will only consider evidence that is relevant to the legal issues in the case.

The court will also consider the legal standards that apply to the case, such as the elements of the claim or defense, and the burden of proof. The moving party must show that there are no genuine issues of material fact and that they are entitled to judgment as a matter of law based on the evidence presented.

The court will view the evidence in the light most favorable to the non-moving party and will draw all reasonable inferences in their favor. If there is a genuine issue of material fact, or if the evidence is not sufficient to support a judgment as a matter of law, the court will deny the motion for summary judgment and the case will proceed to trial.

The main difference between a motion for judgment on the pleadings and a motion for summary judgment is that in a <u>motion</u> for judgment on the pleadings the court only considers the complaint or answer plus any information to which the court can take judicial notice while in a motion for summary judgment the court considers evidence that is beyond what is included in the pleadings.

■ WHY A REQUEST FOR JUDICIAL NOTICE IS IMPORTANT

Judicial notice is a legal procedure that allows a court to accept certain facts as true without requiring formal proof or evidence. Judicial notice is used when a fact is not in dispute or is well-known, and it saves the parties time and resources by avoiding the need to present evidence to prove the fact.

Under the Federal Rules of Evidence and most state rules, a court may take judicial notice of certain facts that are either generally known within the court's territorial jurisdiction or are capable of accurate and ready determination by resorting to sources whose accuracy cannot reasonably be questioned. These facts may include matters of public record, scientific or technical facts, or historical events.

For example, a court may take judicial notice of the fact that a particular law was enacted on a certain date, or that a particular event, such as a hurricane or a presidential election, occurred on a certain date. The court may also take judicial notice of well-known facts, such as the geographic location of a city or the meaning of a common legal term.

Parties may ask the court to take judicial notice of certain facts by filing a motion or request for judicial notice. The request must identify the specific fact or information that the party wants the court to notice and must provide the legal authority and any supporting evidence for the request.

It's important to note that the court has discretion to determine whether to take judicial notice of a particular fact and may consider the parties' objections or arguments before making a ruling. Additionally, taking judicial notice of a fact does not necessarily mean that the fact is conclusive or dispositive of a particular issue in the case.

■ ANTI-SL APP MOTIONS

Be aware of an anti-SLAPP motion. An anti-SLAPP (Strategic Lawsuit Against Public Participation) motion is a legal tool used to dismiss a lawsuit that is aimed at suppressing free speech, such as criticism of public figures or government entities. The effect of an anti-SLAPP motion varies depending on the outcome of the motion.

While anti-SLAPP motions are typically filed in cases where the plaintiff's lawsuit is aimed at suppressing free speech, such as criticism of public figures or government entities, they are also found in a variety of cases. Some examples of the types of cases where anti-SLAPP motions are commonly filed include:

> **Defamation lawsuits**: A defendant may file an anti-SLAPP motion in a defamation lawsuit where the

plaintiff is alleging that the defendant made false statements about them that caused harm to their reputation.

Business disputes: A defendant may file an anti-SLAPP motion in a lawsuit where the plaintiff is alleging that the defendant engaged in unfair competition or made false or misleading statements about their products or services.

Political speech: Anti-SLAPP motions are commonly filed in cases where the plaintiff is a public figure or government entity, and the defendant's speech involves political speech or commentary on matters of public concern.

Employment disputes: In some cases, defendants in employment disputes may file an anti-SLAPP motion if they believe that the plaintiff's lawsuit is aimed at retaliating against them for exercising their right to free speech, such as by reporting workplace violations or expressing their opinions on work-related issues.

■ THE RISK OF ATTORNEY FEES IF AN ANTI-SLAPP MOTION IS GRANTED

If the court grants the anti-SLAPP motion, the lawsuit is dismissed, and the defendant is protected from further legal action. This means that the defendant cannot be sued again for the same speech or conduct, and in most probability will also be entitled to recover their attorneys' fees and costs. If the court denies the anti-SLAPP motion, the lawsuit continues and proceeds to trial.

In this scenario, the defendant will need to continue defending themselves in court against the plaintiff's claims.

Overall, the effect of an anti-SLAPP motion can be significant in protecting free speech and preventing the misuse of the legal system to suppress it. However, the success of an anti-SLAPP motion depends on the specific circumstances of the case, including the applicable laws and the court's interpretation of those laws.

The award of attorney fees is often considered the biggest risk in an anti-SLAPP motion. If the court grants the anti-SLAPP motion and dismisses the lawsuit, the defendant most likely will be awarded a significant amount their attorneys' fees and costs incurred in defending against the lawsuit. However, if the court denies the anti-SLAPP motion, the defendant may be responsible for paying the plaintiff's attorneys' fees and costs, in addition to their own.

The risk of being responsible for the plaintiff's attorneys' fees and costs can be significant, especially in cases where the plaintiff has hired expensive lawyers, or the case has gone on for a long time. The defendants who filed the anti-SLAPP motion and were successful are always awarded attorney fees. If the court determines the defendant's anti-SLAPP motion was frivolous or filed in bad faith the court can award the plaintiff their attorney fees if they were successful in defeating the motion. Therefore, defendants considering filing an anti-SLAPP motion must weigh the potential benefits of the motion against the risk of being responsible for the plaintiff's attorneys' fees and costs if the motion is denied.

It is also worth noting that the award of attorneys' fees in anti-SLAPP motions varies depending on the jurisdiction and the specific circumstances of the case. Some jurisdictions may require the plaintiff to show that the defendant's speech or conduct was made with malice or in bad faith before awarding attorneys' fees to the plaintiff, while other jurisdictions may have different standards.

■ LEGAL MEMO

The next thing to do is prepare a legal memo of the case. A memo gives an analysis of the case, identifying the legal theories, the key issues, and the potential defenses. One of the best ways to identify the legal theories is to go through the standard jury instructions. These instructions set forth all of the elements of each of your legal theories and what you have to prove.

You'll want to look at the documents in the case, interview people, and do some legal research early on to determine whether you have a viable claim. Once you have done all that research, then you are going to go about drafting the complaint, if you are representing the plaintiffs. Drafting a complaint is especially important because if you plead something in your complaint and at a later time, you want to change what you have pled, it is possible that the court can prevent you from doing that. The court may not allow you to amend the complaint if you have made something that is referred to as a judicial admission. You must be careful when you are drafting a complaint.

CHAPTER 6

CREATING A DISCOVERY PLAN

Sometimes you come across attorneys who never go to trial. They file lawsuits and engage in extensive discovery without a clear purpose but settle all their cases before trial to avoid presenting their case before a jury. A true trial lawyer is an attorney who plans on going to trial at the time he or she files their complaint.

An attorney who does not do discovery is exposing himself to legal malpractice. You have a certain duty to represent your client as zealously as you can, and that often entails engaging in discovery. Doing discovery sometimes can even shorten the required trial time. It is important to have a discovery plan.

If your client insists that he does not want you to spend a lot of money on discovery, then you need to put that into a document to show that you have advised your client of the kind of discovery you believe is needed, and the risk involved in not doing it. If things do not go well at the trial and the client tries to blame you, you then have something in writing, stating that you advised your client of the need to engage in a discovery plan.

■ KNOW YOUR THEORY OF THE CASE

A true trial attorney will prepare a discovery plan. Before you can create a discovery plan, you need to develop your theory of the case. A theory of a case could be simply a couple of sentences or short paragraphs of what you would tell the jury about your case and why you should prevail. In order to prove your theory of the case, you have to develop a discovery plan to prove all these points with evidence.

A discovery plan is a process for gathering information and data about a particular subject or problem. Before you begin, you need to determine what you hope to achieve with your discovery plan. There are several reasons to conduct discovery. One critical purpose of discovery is to gather information about the case.

Not what you already know but other information that you may need to present at trial. For example, if your case concerns defective construction or a construction delay damage claim you may want the building permits and inspection records issued by the Department of Building and Safety.

This will show whether the project passed inspection on various days and by which trades. This can be obtained by serving a deposition subpoena on the Department of Building and Safety with a request for the production of business records.

■ WHAT TO ACCOMPLISH WITH DISCOVERY

Another reason to engage in discovery is to find out what your opposition already knows so that you are prepared to deal with it at the time of trial and you want to pin down their position, so it does not change when you get to trial.

Sometimes you engage in discovery to preserve the evidence if a witness becomes unavailable at the time of trial. You do this by taking a deposition of a party who may be elderly, suffers from health issues, or otherwise may not be available to attend the trial in the future.

Your discovery plan should identify your sources of information and determine where you can gather your needed information. This might include research papers, books, online sources, interviews, and surveys. You must also create a timeline for your discovery plan. This will help you stay on track and ensure that you have enough time to gather all the necessary information.

Conduct appropriate research. Use your chosen sources to gather information about your subject. Take detailed notes and keep track of any important findings. Once you have gathered your information, organize it in a way that makes sense to you. You might use charts, tables, or graphs to visualize your findings. Look for patterns and trends in your data. This will help you draw conclusions and make informed decisions.

Finally write up a summary of your findings. This should include any important conclusions or recommendations and share your findings with others who may benefit from them. This might include colleagues, clients, or stakeholders.

An important development in the discovery process, over the last several years, is electronically stored information. These days, a lot of litigation involves obtaining emails or documents that were posted on social media. A lot of times, in extraordinarily complex litigation, there could be a million digital documents. It becomes a challenge to catalog and manage those documents. There are now companies that offer a platform that allows you to upload not only documents that are scanned, but also original native documents, to establish an overly complex database and be able to search by criteria to locate documents.

■ DISCOVERY METHODS

Interrogatories

Interrogatories are a type of discovery tool that can be used in a legal case to obtain information from the opposing party. Interrogatories are written questions that are sent to the other party, and they must be answered under oath within a specified time frame.

In civil cases, interrogatories are often used to obtain information about the opposing party's claims or defenses, as well as to gather information about witnesses, documents, and other evidence.

Interrogatories are typically limited in number, and the questions must be relevant to the case and not overly burdensome or intrusive. The party receiving the interrogatories has a duty to respond truthfully and completely, and failure to do so can result in sanctions or penalties.

The best use of interrogatories is to get answers to questions that you cannot normally get by taking a party's deposition. For example, if an issue in your case is to find out the amount of sales your opponent made of a product (Widget) during the years 2013-2016 that answer may take a detailed review of past sales records. The best way to get that information is by an interrogatory because a witness at a deposition may not know that answer to that question off the top of his or her head. The answer can only be found by examining business records. Keep in mind the attorney for the witness normally prepares the answers to interrogatories and often times tries to obstruct your ability to gather this information. If that happens you need to file a motion with the court to compel the answer to that specific interrogatory. If a witness at a deposition does not answer the question because he or she just does not know without looking at documents, there is no point making a motion to compel that witness to answer a question to which he or she does not know the answer.

Depositions

Depositions can be an effective tool in a legal case, as they allow attorneys to gather evidence and information that can be used to build a case or to impeach witnesses during trial. From my experience, depositions are the most powerful and important discovery technique. The other discovery methods usually allow the attorney to prepare and sanitize the response. In a deposition you have the opposing party or key witness answering questions in real time.

During a deposition, a witness is placed under oath and asked questions by the opposing attorney, with a court reporter present to record the testimony. The testimony can be used to support or challenge claims made by either side in the case. Some of the potential benefits of depositions include:

> **Gathering evidence**: Depositions can provide an opportunity for attorneys to gather evidence and information that may not be available through other means, such as written documents or witness statements.

> **Assessing witness credibility**: Depositions can allow attorneys to assess the credibility and reliability of witnesses, as they can observe their demeanor, tone, and body language during questioning.

> **Impeachment at trial**: Deposition testimony can be used to impeach a witness during trial if their

testimony at trial differs from their earlier deposition testimony.

However, there are also potential drawbacks to depositions, such as the time and expense involved in conducting them, as well as the risk that a witness may provide testimony that is harmful to one's case.

The opposing counsel representing their client or deponent who is giving deposition testimony often tries to disrupt the process by stating repetitive and improper objections and instructing the deponent not to answer a question. It's a recipe for a contentious deposition.

An attorney cannot properly instruct a witness not to answer a question at a deposition. The only exception is if the question violates a privilege like an attorney-client privilege. If a question is objectionable but does not infringe upon a privilege, the attorney can only state an objection on the record to preserve their objection for trial. The witness must then answer the question.

At a trial, only relevant evidence is admissible. Relevant evidence is evidence that tends to make the existence of a fact that is of consequence to the case more or less probable than it would be without the evidence. In other words, relevant evidence is evidence that is logically connected to a fact that is at issue in the case and that tends to either support or undermine that fact.

For example, if the fact at issue in a case is whether a defendant was present at the scene of a crime, evidence that relates to the defendant's whereabouts at the time of the crime would be relevant. On the other hand, evidence that is unrelated to the defendant's whereabouts, such as information about the defendant's family background or personal habits, would not be relevant.

The concept of relevance is important in the legal system, as it helps to ensure that only evidence that is related to the issues at hand is admitted in court. This helps to prevent the introduction of irrelevant or prejudicial evidence that could potentially bias the jury or lead to an unfair outcome.

During the discovery phase of the case, parties are allowed to inquire into evidence that may not be relevant at trial but is likely to lead to the discovery of admissible evidence that could be used at trial.

For example, it is appropriate to ask a witness about a conversation with another person even though that conversation would be hearsay and not admissible at trial. By giving great latitude during discovery the attorney can learn of a potential witness who was participant in that conversation.

If the questioning attorney is engaging in inappropriate behavior in his questioning the other attorney can request the deposition is stopped and move for a protective order. A protective order is a court order that limits or prohibits certain actions or behavior by one or more parties in a legal case. In the context of a deposition, a protective order may be sought if a party believes that certain behavior by another party during the deposition is inappropriate or disruptive.

Some of the grounds for seeking a protective order for behavior at a deposition may include:

Harassment: If one party is engaging in harassing behavior towards another party, such as making threats or using abusive language, a protective order may be sought to prohibit such behavior.

Intimidation: If one party is engaging in behavior that is intended to intimidate or coerce another party or witness, such as invading personal space or making physical gestures, a protective order may be sought.

If one party is refusing to answer relevant questions during the deposition or is providing evasive or non-responsive answers, the attorney may file a motion with the court for an order to compel that witness to provide complete and truthful answers.

If a party files a motion for a protective order, the court will impose sanctions against the party losing that motion. The courts do not like discovery disputes and are quick to sanction parties who do not act in good faith to resolve discovery disputes.

■ REQUEST FOR ADMISSIONS OF THE TRUTH OF FACTS OR THE AUTHENTICATION OF DOCUMENTS

A Request for Admissions is a formal legal request made by one party in a legal proceeding to the other party for them to admit or deny certain facts or statements that are relevant to the case. This request is typically made during the discovery phase of a legal proceeding, where each side is required to disclose evidence and information they have that is relevant to the case.

The purpose of a Request for Admissions is to narrow the issues in dispute by identifying facts that both parties agree on and by compelling the opposing party to admit or deny certain facts or statements. This can streamline the legal proceeding by avoiding the need to present evidence on issues that are not in dispute.

A Request for Admissions is typically made in writing and must be served to the other party. The other party has a specified amount of time to respond to the request by admitting or denying each statement or fact. If the other party fails to respond or fails to admit or deny a statement, the statement is considered admitted. If the other party admits to a statement or fact, it is considered a binding admission for the purpose of the case. If the other party denies a statement or fact, the requesting party may need to provide evidence to prove the statement or fact.

A Request for Admissions is the only discovery method where the answer is conclusively established without the need for further proof or evidence. A major difference between a Request for Admission and any other discovery method like a deposition or an answer to an interrogatory, is that an answer to an interrogatory or an answer at a deposition, while given under oath, is not conclusively established.

At trial, the party that gave that prior answer could testify differently at trial. The consequence is that he or she would be subject to impeachment, which the jury can consider in assessing that parties' credibility.

It's important to note that the requesting party must properly frame their Requests for Admissions to ensure that the admissions obtained are relevant and useful to the case. The admitting party also has the opportunity to explain or qualify their admissions if they believe that there are mitigating circumstances or additional information that should be considered.

Overall, a Request for Admissions can be a powerful tool in legal proceedings, allowing each party to streamline the issues in dispute and potentially avoid the need for time-consuming and expensive discovery methods.

■ JUDICIAL ADMISSIONS

While a judicial admission is not a discovery technique it is an important legal principle. Judicial admissions are statements or facts that a party admits to during the course of litigation, either through pleadings, testimony, or other means. Unlike admissions made in response to a Request for Admissions, judicial admissions are made voluntarily by the party and are binding on that party for the remainder of the case.

Judicial admissions can be used in several ways during litigation. First, they can be used as evidence to support a party's claims or defenses. For example, if a plaintiff admits in their complaint that they were injured in a car accident, that admission can be used as evidence to support their claim for damages.

Second, judicial admissions can be used to narrow the issues in dispute. If a party admits to certain facts or statements, those issues are no longer in dispute, and the parties can focus their efforts on other issues that remain contested.

Finally, judicial admissions can be used to prevent a party from contradicting their earlier statements or testimony. For example, if a defendant admits during a deposition that they were present at the scene of an accident, they cannot later deny that fact at trial without exposing themselves to charges of perjury.

Overall, judicial admissions can be a powerful tool in litigation, allowing parties to streamline the issues in dispute, provide evidence in support of their claims or defenses, and prevent parties from contradicting their earlier statements or testimony.

■ REQUEST FOR PRODUCTION AND INSPECTION OF DOCUMENTS

You should always send out a request for production of documents early in the litigation. A Request for Production of Documents is a formal legal request made by one party in a legal dispute with the other party to produce certain documents or other tangible things that are relevant to the case. This request can be made during the discovery phase of a legal proceeding, where each side is required to disclose the evidence and information they have that is relevant to the case.

The documents requested may include things like contracts, correspondence, emails, invoices, receipts, financial statements, medical records, or any other type of document that may be relevant to the case. The party making the request must specify the documents or items that they are seeking with enough detail to enable the other party to identify and locate the documents.

Once a Request for Production of Documents is made, the other party must respond within a specified period of time, either by producing the requested documents or by objecting to the request if they believe it is not valid or too broad.

A Request for Production of Documents is important because it allows each party to gather the evidence and information they need to build their case. By obtaining relevant documents and tangible items, each party can gain a better understanding of the facts of the case, assess the strengths and weaknesses of their position, and prepare their arguments and strategies for trial or settlement negotiations.

Additionally, a Request for Production of Documents helps to ensure that each party has access to all the relevant evidence and information, and that there are no surprises at trial. This promotes fairness and transparency in the legal process and allows each party to make informed decisions about their case.

A Request for Production of Documents can help to narrow the issues in dispute and potentially facilitate settlement negotiations. If one party produces documents that are particularly damaging to their case, for example, it may encourage them to consider settling the case rather than proceeding to trial.

If a party fails to produce documents in response to a Request for Production of Documents, there are several remedies available to the other party. These remedies may vary depending on the specific rules and procedures of the court in which the case is being heard, but generally include:

Motion to Compel: The party who made the request can file a motion to compel the other party to produce the requested documents. This motion asks the court to order the other party to comply with the request and produce the documents.

Sanctions: The court may impose sanctions on the party who failed to produce the requested documents. Sanctions can include fines, attorney's fees, or even the striking of pleadings or dismissal of the case.

Adverse Inference: If the party who failed to produce the requested documents had control over the documents and failed to produce them without a valid excuse, the court may allow the other party to use that failure as evidence against them at trial. This is known as an adverse inference.

Contempt of Court: If a party willfully disobeys a court order to produce documents, the court may hold them in contempt of court, which can result in fines or even imprisonment.

A Request for Production of Documents is a critical tool in the discovery process of a legal proceeding, allowing each party to gather and review the evidence and information necessary to effectively pursue their case.

■ DEMAND FOR INSPECTION OF PREMISES

A Demand for Inspection of Premises is a formal legal request made by one party in a legal dispute to the other party for permission to enter and inspect a property or premises that is relevant to the case. This request is typically made during the discovery phase of a legal proceeding, where each side is required to disclose the evidence and information they have that is relevant to the case.

The purpose of a Demand for Inspection of Premises is to allow the requesting party to gather evidence and information about the condition of the property or premises, as well as any other relevant information that may be obtained through inspection. This may include things like taking measurements, photographs, or video recordings of the property, examining the condition of the property, or identifying any hazards or risks that may be present.

A Demand for Inspection of Premises must be made in writing and served to the other party, and must specify the date, time, and location of the proposed inspection. The other party has the right to object to the inspection if they believe it is not necessary or if it would be unduly burdensome, but if the court approves the request, the other party must allow the inspection to take place.

■ DEMAND FOR PHYSICAL OR MENTAL EXAMINATION

A Demand for a Physical or Mental Examination is a formal legal request made by one party in a lawsuit to the other party for permission to have the opposing party undergo a medical examination. This request is typically made during the discovery phase of a lawsuit and is used when a party's physical or mental condition is at issue in the case.

The purpose of a Demand for a Physical or Mental Examination is to allow the requesting party to obtain objective medical evidence about the opposing party's physical or mental condition. This may include things like a physical examination, psychological evaluation, or other medical tests that are relevant to the case.

The requesting party must demonstrate to the court that the examination is necessary and relevant to the case. The court will consider factors such as the nature of the case, the specific medical issues at stake, and the potential impact of the examination on the privacy and dignity of the opposing party. If the court approves the request, the opposing party must undergo the examination by a qualified medical professional. The results of the examination may be used as evidence in the case.

A Demand for a Physical or Mental Examination is an important tool in a lawsuit, allowing each party to obtain objective medical evidence about the physical or mental condition of the opposing party. This can be particularly important in cases where the opposing party's condition is a central issue in the case, such as personal injury lawsuits or disability claims.

CHAPTER 7

JURY SELECTION

J ury selection is a crucial component of litigation, as it involves the process of selecting a group of individuals to serve as jurors in a trial. We often hear the goal of jury selection is to choose a group of impartial jurors who can hear evidence and render a fair and impartial verdict based on the facts presented in the case. That is not necessarily the case. If you could seat twelve clones of your client in the jury panel that would be ideal from your perspective. Who better to decide your case than twelve identical copies of your client. However, since we have an adversarial system of justice, and both sides have input on the jurors that will hear the case with the opportunity to reject some jurors, the system seems to work.

The jury selection process is governed by both federal and state laws and varies from jurisdiction to jurisdiction. In general, the process begins with the selection of a pool of potential jurors from the community in which the trial will take place. This pool is typically selected from a list of registered voters, licensed drivers, or individuals with state-issued identification cards.

Once the pool of potential jurors is selected, the court will usually summon them to appear for jury duty. During this process, potential jurors are typically required to complete a questionnaire that provides information about their background, education, employment, and other factors that may be relevant to their ability to serve as impartial jurors.

After the completion of the questionnaire, the court will typically conduct a process called voir dire which involves questioning potential jurors to determine their suitability to serve on the jury. During voir dire, both the plaintiff and defense attorneys, as well as the judge, will have the opportunity to question potential jurors about their background, beliefs, and experiences that may impact their ability to serve as impartial jurors.

When you watch the jury come in, you can see the people who are the more dominant ones; the ones who seem like leaders. You want to be able to identify those people.

In jury selection a "lion" is a potential juror who is considered to be strong-willed, assertive, or outspoken while a "lamb" is considered a potential juror who is perceived as meek, submissive, or easily swayed by the opinions of others.

You want to have at least one lion on your panel that believes in the theory of your case and is receptive to your position. You don't need to care how many lambs are on your side because these lions basically corral the lambs and get them to think the same way that they think. I'd be careful of having too many lions and you certainly don't want a lion on your panel who is going to be opposed to your case. When you are going through the selection of jurors, there are different theories on how you can go about the process.

CHAPTER 8

THEORIES: HOW JURIES DECIDE CASES

■ THE JUROR'S PERSPECTIVE

Everybody has a collection of bias, fears, values, experiences, and other personal characteristics that is often referred to as their "perspective," "world view," or "schema." This refers to the individual's unique way of understanding and interpreting the world around them, based on their personal history, culture, beliefs, and other factors.

Perspective plays a significant role in how people perceive and interact with the world, and can influence their attitudes, behaviors, and decisions. Understanding and acknowledging the diversity of perspectives that exist within a community or society is an important aspect of promoting empathy, inclusivity, and effective communication.

The nature of the decision-making process is the filtering of the evidence through the juror's schema. Depending on the jurors' attitudes on the particular subject, the juror remembers and believes the evidence that supports their perspective and ignores and rejects the evidence that is contrary to their perspective.

■ THE ROLE OF COGNITIVE DISSONANCE

The psychological process known as cognitive dissonance plays a role in resolving any conflict the juror may have between the evidence they hear and their perspective on the particular topic. Cognitive dissonance refers to the mental discomfort experienced by an individual when they hold two or more contradictory beliefs or values or when their beliefs and behaviors are not aligned.

The theory of cognitive dissonance suggests that when individuals encounter situations that conflict with their beliefs or values, they experience a state of psychological discomfort or tension. This discomfort motivates them to reduce the dissonance by changing their beliefs, attitudes, or behaviors in order to restore consistency.

For example, if someone believes that smoking is harmful but still smokes, they may experience cognitive dissonance because their behavior contradicts their belief. To reduce the dissonance, they may either quit smoking or convince themselves that smoking is not as harmful as they previously believed.

Cognitive dissonance can have important implications for behavior change, persuasion, and decision-making. By understanding cognitive dissonance, individuals can better understand why they may resist change or cling to their beliefs even in the face of evidence to the contrary.

Jurors evaluate facts based upon their individual perspective. They take their perception of the facts into the deliberations and resolve any conflict through the process of cognitive dissonance.

During deliberations when a juror is presented with facts that conflict with their "schema" they twist or skew those facts to resolve that conflict and then create a story in their mind to explain and justify their decision. Once an individual develops their "schema" on a particular subject they fight like mad to preserve that belief and go to great lengths to resolve any conflict that challenges their established belief system.

■ SCHEMA THEORY IN JURY DECISION MAKING

The Schema Theory was developed by social psychologists and is considered a prominent theory in understanding juror behavior.[2] The Schema Theory suggests that jurors rely on pre-existing mental frameworks or "schemas" to process information and reach a verdict. These schemas are developed through a juror's prior experiences, knowledge, and beliefs, and can influence how they interpret evidence and make judgments about the defendant's guilt or innocence.

Under the Schema Theory there is no such thing as a neutral fact and jurors are not passive receptacles of information presented to them during the trial. Instead, each fact, whether it appears "neutral" or not passes through the jurors *filtering* mechanism. These filtering mechanisms are constructed from each person's preexisting attitudes, beliefs, feelings, values, experiences, and needs both cognitive and emotional dispositions. Under the filtering process evidence is presented to the jury —passes through the juror's perception of the facts — goes through the deliberations — and results in the verdict.

The Schema Theory helps people deal with all the incoming information by placing great deference to information that meets with their schema, filtering out information that challenges their schema

---

[2] Tieger, *A Summary of Recently Conducted Behavioral Research;* Levine *Jury Selection* (2004) section 4:34

and drawing inferences about what happened that led to the litigation they are perceiving. The jurors then use their schema to remember, interpret, organize, and explain what happened in a story they use in rendering their verdict.[3]

According to the Schema Theory, jurors use schemas to categorize and organize information presented during a trial, allowing them to make sense of complex and often ambiguous evidence. For example, a juror may have a schema for what constitutes "reasonable doubt," which they use to evaluate the prosecution's case and determine if there is sufficient evidence to convict the defendant.

However, the Schema Theory also suggests that jurors may rely on stereotypes or biases in their decision making, particularly if those biases are relevant to the case. For example, a juror who holds negative stereotypes about a particular racial or ethnic group may be more likely to find a defendant from that group guilty, even if the evidence does not support that conclusion.

Schema Theory suggests that individuals have mental frameworks or structures of knowledge that organize and interpret information in the world around them. These structures, or schemas, help people understand new information by providing a framework for categorizing and interpreting it.

In terms of story formation, Schema Theory suggests that individuals use their existing schemas to create mental models of the characters, setting, and events in a story. These mental models help individuals make sense of the story and anticipate what will happen next. As new information is introduced, individuals may revise their mental models to incorporate this new information.

Overall, the Schema Theory suggests that juror decision making

---

[3] *see Moore Trial by Schema: Cognitive Filters; Levine On Trial Advocacy (2004) Chapter 4.8*

is influenced by a combination of cognitive processes, prior knowledge and experiences, and the social context of the trial. As such, efforts to improve jury decision making may involve addressing biases and promoting more rational and evidence-based decision-making strategies.

Other theories on how juries decide cases is by looking at the personality traits of jurors and heuristics which examines bias.

CHAPTER 9

PERSONALITY TRAITS OF JURORS

After you examine jurors using the Schema Theory, you need to also consider the juror's personality traits. The personality traits of jurors can have an impact on how they perceive evidence and how they ultimately decide a case.

Research has shown that certain personality traits can help predict the decision-making process of jurors. Some of the key personality traits that have been studied in relation to jury decision-making include:

> **Openness to experience**: Jurors who score high on openness to experience may be more willing to consider new and unconventional ideas presented in the trial. This trait could make them more receptive to novel legal arguments or testimony from unconventional witnesses.

Conscientiousness: Jurors who score high on conscientiousness may be more likely to carefully consider all of the evidence presented in the case and may be more diligent in their deliberations. This trait could make them more detail-oriented and less likely to jump to conclusions.

Agreeableness: Jurors who score high on agreeableness may be more likely to be swayed by the opinions of their fellow jurors or by the emotional appeals made by attorneys in the case. This trait could make them more empathetic to the parties involved and may make them more likely to seek a compromise or a consensus.

Neuroticism: Jurors who score high on neuroticism may be more prone to feelings of anxiety or emotional distress during the trial. This trait could make them more likely to be influenced by their emotions or to be biased by their own experiences.

Extraversion: Jurors who score high on extraversion may be more likely to engage in discussions with their fellow jurors and may be more willing to speak up and share their opinions. This trait could make them more vocal in their deliberations and more likely to advocate for their positions.

Social scientists have discovered connections between certain well-defined personality traits and the manner in which jurors perceive and decide cases. There are several sets of alternative personality traits to consider based upon the type of case.

■ AFFECTIVE VS. COGNITIVE

According to Dr. Donald E. Vison, a recognized expert in jury selection, most jurors can be identified as either a "cognitive" or "affective" personality. A cognitive personality makes decisions based upon reason while an affective personality makes decisions on emotions. In some cases, you may want a juror who has a cognitive personality, in others you may prefer an affective personality who is swayed by emotion.

■ COGNITIVE PERSONALITY TRAITS

Cognitive personality traits are dimensions of personality that describe how individuals tend to think, reason, and process information. These traits can influence an individual's decision-making process and how they evaluate evidence in a trial. People with cognitive personality traits display a high level of intelligence.

This trait describes an individual's ability to learn, reason, and solve problems. Individuals who score high on intelligence tend to be more analytical, logical, and detail-oriented in their thinking. Cognitive personalities also have a level of organization, responsibility, and discipline. People with this trait tend to be more reliable and focused on their thinking and decision-making. They enjoy engaging in complex cognitive tasks and may be more likely to carefully consider evidence presented in a trial.

Cognitive personality traits can influence how jurors process and evaluate evidence presented in a trial. For example, jurors who show an openness to experience may be more likely to consider complex legal arguments or scientific evidence presented in a trial. Understanding these personality traits can help attorneys and jury consultants better predict and understand juror behavior and decision-making processes.

Cognitive personality traits are often valued in many types of jobs or professions that require analytical thinking, problem-solving, and decision-making skills. Some examples of professions that may attract individuals with high levels of cognitive personality traits include people working in:

Science and research: Individuals with high levels of cognitive personality traits, such as intelligence and openness to experience, may be attracted to careers in scientific research, where they can engage in complex problem-solving and analysis.

Law and legal professions: The legal profession often requires individuals with high levels of cognitive personality traits, such as conscientiousness and need for cognition, who are able to evaluate complex legal arguments and evidence.

Engineering and technology: Careers in engineering and technology often require individuals with high levels of cognitive personality traits, such as intelligence and problem-solving skills, who can design and develop innovative solutions to complex problems.

Finance and accounting: The finance and accounting professions require individuals with high levels of cognitive personality traits, such as attention to detail and conscientiousness, who are able to analyze complex financial data and make sound financial decisions.

Psychology: Cognitive personality traits such as openness, conscientiousness, extraversion, agreeableness, and neuroticism are found in psychologists. Psychologists may use case studies, personal anecdotes, and real-world examples to illustrate these traits.

Education: Educators may use storytelling, role-playing, and group discussions to explore cognitive traits such as critical thinking, creativity, and problem- solving.

Marketing: Marketers may use focus groups, surveys, and social media to explore cognitive traits such as motivation, decision-making, and brand loyalty.

Medicine and healthcare: Healthcare professions require individuals with high levels of cognitive personality traits, such as intelligence and problem- solving skills, who can diagnose and treat complex medical conditions and make critical decisions about patient care.

However, it is important to note that cognitive personality traits can be found in individuals across many different professions and industries, and that these traits are not limited to any specific type of job or profession.

A cognitive personality may be somebody who majored in business, math, accounting, bookkeeping, or physical science. They may take jobs like electricians, mechanics, or carpenters. They will often be intellectually controlled. It is not always easy to tell if a prospective juror has a particular personality trait. Here are the types of case and some voir dire questions that can spot a cognitive personality trait.

■ CASES IN WHICH YOU MAY WANT A COGNITIVE PERSONALITY

A cognitive personality might be particularly useful in cases where the focus is on understanding complex information or reasoning. For example, in cases involving patents, copyrights, or trademarks, a cognitive personality would be valuable in understanding complex technical or legal concepts and applying them to the case.

In cases involving allegations of insider trading or other financial misconduct, a cognitive personality would be useful in understanding complex financial statements, market data, and regulatory frameworks.

In cases involving allegations of medical negligence, a cognitive personality would be helpful in understanding medical jargon, scientific studies, and complex medical procedures.

In cases involving allegations of discrimination or harassment, a cognitive personality would be useful in understanding the nuances of language, culture, and social dynamics that underlie these issues.

In cases involving allegations of pollution or other environmental harms, a cognitive personality would be valuable in understanding complex scientific data, environmental regulations, and environmental policy.

In general, any case that involves complex technical, legal, or scientific information would benefit from a juror who has a strong cognitive ability. Such jurors would be better equipped to understand the evidence presented and make informed decisions based on the facts of the case.

These are just some of the factors to consider and the use of personality trait is a heuristic used as a short-cut in choosing a juror. Remember depending on which side you represent you may want an affective personality.

■ VOIR DIRE QUESTIONS TO SPOT A COGNITIVE PERSONALITY

During voir dire you can spot a cognitive personality with carefully crafted questions. Here are some examples:

- How do you approach decision-making in your personal and professional life?
- Do you tend to analyze all the available information and weigh the pros and cons before deciding, or do you make decisions based on intuition or gut feelings?
- Are you willing to consider multiple perspectives and viewpoints when deciding, or do you tend to stick to your own beliefs and opinions?
- How do you handle situations where you are presented with conflicting information or viewpoints?
- Do you consider yourself to be a detail-oriented person? How do you ensure that you have a full understanding of all the facts and evidence before deciding?
- How do you approach problem-solving and decision-making? Do you tend to rely on logic and reason, or do you make decisions based on emotions or personal biases?
- Are you interested in learning new things and expanding your knowledge? How do you stay informed about current events and issues that may be relevant to this case?

■ AFFECTIVE PERSONALITY TRAITS

Affective personality traits can also influence how jurors make decisions in a trial. For example, jurors who score high on traits such as empathy and emotional intelligence may be more likely to consider the emotional impact of the evidence and how it may affect the parties involved.

Neuroticism

This trait describes an individual's tendency to experience negative emotions such as anxiety, fear, and anger. Jurors who score high on neuroticism may be more likely to be swayed by emotional appeals and may have a harder time evaluating evidence objectively.

Agreeableness

This trait describes an individual's tendency to be cooperative, compassionate, and empathetic towards others. Jurors who score high on agreeableness may be more likely to empathize with the parties involved in the case and may be more likely to seek a compromise or a peaceful resolution.

Extraversion

This trait describes an individual's tendency to be outgoing, sociable, and assertive. Jurors who score high on extraversion may be more likely to express their opinions and influence the opinions of others during jury deliberations.

Conscientiousness

This trait describes an individual's tendency to be organized, responsible, and disciplined. Jurors who score high on conscientiousness may be more likely to take their duties as jurors seriously and may be more likely to carefully consider the evidence presented.

Understanding the affective personality traits of jurors can help attorneys and jury consultants better predict and understand juror behavior and decision-making processes. However, it is important to note that individual differences in affective personality traits may interact with other factors, such as the specific details of the case, to influence juror decision-making in complex and nuanced ways.

Affective personality traits are dimensions of personality that describe how individuals tend to experience and express emotions in different situations. These traits are sometimes referred to as emotional traits and are thought to be relatively stable across time and situations. Some professions or jobs that may attract individuals with high levels of affective personality traits include:

Counseling and social work: Individuals with high levels of affective personality traits, such as empathy and emotional intelligence, may be drawn to careers in counseling and social work, where they can help others manage their emotions and navigate difficult situations.

Teaching and education: Teaching and education often require individuals with high levels of affective personality traits, such as patience and compassion, who are able to connect with students and create a positive learning environment.

Performing arts and entertainment: Careers in the performing arts and entertainment industry may attract individuals with high levels of affective personality traits, such as extroversion and openness to experience, who enjoy expressing themselves creatively and entertaining others.

Healthcare and nursing: Healthcare and nursing professions require individuals with high levels of affective personality traits, such as compassion and empathy, who can provide emotional support and care for patients.

Human resources and management: Individuals with high levels of affective personality traits, such as emotional intelligence and interpersonal skills, may excel in careers in human resources and management, where they can effectively manage and motivate employees and foster positive work environments.

■ CASES IN WHICH YOU MAY WANT AN AFFECTIVE PERSONALITY

An affective personality might be particularly useful in cases where the focus is on emotional or psychological issues. For example, in cases involving physical or emotional harm, an affective personality would be valuable in understanding the emotional and psychological impact of the injury on the victim, and in empathizing with their suffering.

In cases involving custody disputes, an affective personality would be helpful in understanding the emotional needs of the child and the impact that different custody arrangements would have on the child's well-being.

In cases involving allegations of sexual assault, an affective personality would be useful in understanding the trauma and emotional impact of the assault on the victim, and in empathizing with their experience.

In cases involving the death of a loved one, an affective personality would be valuable in understanding the emotional impact of the loss on the family members, and in empathizing with their grief.

In cases involving allegations of discrimination or harassment, an affective personality would be useful in understanding the emotional impact of the discrimination on the victim, and in empathizing with their experience.

In general, any case that involves emotional or psychological issues would benefit from a juror who has a strong affective ability. Such jurors would be better equipped to understand the emotional impact of the case on the parties involved and make decisions that are compassionate and just.

■ VOIR DIRE QUESTIONS TO SPOT AN AFFECTIVE PERSONALITY

Do you believe it's important to consider the feelings and emotions of others when making decisions? Have you ever been in a situation where you had to empathize with someone who had a different perspective than you?

Have you ever been the victim of a crime or a similar situation? Do you have any personal grievances against the defendant or the justice system? How do you typically react when you feel angry or resentful?

Do you tend to worry a lot or feel anxious in stressful situations? Have you ever been in a situation where you had to make a difficult decision while feeling anxious or worried? Have you ever suffered from depression or experienced a period of sadness or hopelessness? How did you cope with these feelings?

Have you ever been in a situation where you felt afraid for your safety or the safety of others? Do you have any concerns or fears related to this case or the defendant? Have you ever been in a situation where you felt guilty or responsible for something that happened? How did you handle these feelings? Do you believe that the justice system is fair and effective? Have you ever felt that your efforts would be futile in a particular situation?

■ AUTHORITARIAN VS. ANTI-AUTHORITARIAN

The authoritarian versus the anti-authoritarian personality trait may be the most revealing personality trait to predict the outcome of a jury trial.

The authoritarian personality trait is characterized by a tendency to submit to authority, to be rigid in one's beliefs, and to prefer social order and control. Research has suggested that individuals who score high on the authoritarian personality trait may be more likely to favor prosecution and conviction in a jury trial. Studies have shown that jurors with high levels of authoritarianism may be more likely to:

- Believe that law enforcement officers are generally honest and trustworthy and may be more likely to accept their testimony and evidence without question. Be more punitive and less empathetic towards defendants, particularly those who are perceived as violating social norms or threatening social order.
- Be more likely to rely on stereotypes and preconceived notions about defendants, particularly those who are members of marginalized or stigmatized groups. Be less open to new information and less likely to change their minds during deliberation.

Political conservatism can be an indication of an authoritarian personality. During voir dire ask if the prospective juror considers themself to be politically conservative or tends toward being more of a liberal ideology.

People with authoritarian personality traits might be antagonistic toward persons perceived to be of lower status including showing a prejudice against minorities of lower socioeconomic groups.

Authoritarian personalities are concerned with the status of in-dividuals. If you are defending a case where the plaintiff has a low social status suing a respected large corporation you will want a juror with an authoritarian personality on your jury.

You can often spot an authoritarian personality when you first observe them upon entering the courtroom on the first day of trial. They may be dressed for jury duty wearing a suit and tie and will show great deference to the judge.

By contrast, anti-authoritarian personalities show tolerance of dissent, support for persons of low power or prestige, a willingness to forgive and understand deviance, a high regard for individualism, and a belief in social responsibility.

It is important to note that authoritarian personality traits are not necessarily linked to specific types of jobs, as individuals with these traits can be found in various professions. However, certain jobs may attract individuals with authoritarian tendencies, such as:

Law enforcement: Police officers and other law enforcement personnel often require a strong sense of authority and discipline. Individuals with authoritarian personality traits may be drawn to this type of work.

Military: Similarly, the military requires individuals who are disciplined and able to follow orders. Authoritarian personality traits may be beneficial in this context.

Politics: Politicians with authoritarian tendencies may be drawn to positions of power and control, where they can exercise authority over others.

Corporate leadership: Authoritarian personality traits may be beneficial in positions of corporate leadership, where individuals need to be decisive and assertive.

Education: While it may seem counterintuitive, some individuals with authoritarian tendencies may be drawn to teaching positions, where they can exert control over students and their behavior.

■ CASES IN WHICH YOU MAY WANT AN AUTHORITARIAN PERSONALITY

An authoritarian personality is characterized by a strong belief in authority, obedience, and strict adherence to rules and regulations. An authoritarian personality may be more suited to certain types of cases where a strict interpretation of rules and adherence to authority is critical. Some examples include, in cases involving military personnel who have violated military law or regulations, an authoritarian personality may be better suited to understand the importance of strict adherence to military protocols and discipline.

In cases involving complex financial crimes or fraud, an authoritarian personality may be more likely to view the alleged actions as black-and-white and less likely to consider mitigating factors such as intent or extenuating circumstances.

In cases involving immigration violations, an authoritarian personality may be more likely to view the need for strict enforcement of immigration laws and regulations as paramount, rather than considering the human impact of deportation or other consequences.

In cases involving alleged threats to public safety, such as terrorism or mass shootings, an authoritarian personality may be more likely to prioritize the need for strict security measures and swift punishment for those involved.

■ VOIR DIRE QUESTIONS TO SPOT AN AUTHORITARIAN PERSONALITY

Here are some potential voir dire questions that could help identify jurors who may have an authoritarian personality:

- Do you believe that rules and regulations should always be followed, even if they seem unfair or unnecessary?
- Have you ever had a job or role where you were responsible for enforcing rules or regulations? How did you approach that responsibility?
- Do you believe that people who break the law should always be punished, regardless of the circumstances or intent behind their actions? How do you feel about authority figures, such as police officers or military personnel? Do you have a great deal of respect for them, or do you question their decisions or motives?
- Are there any circumstances where you believe it is appropriate to disobey the law or authority figures? If so, what are those circumstances?
- Do you believe that there are certain groups of people who are more likely to break the law or engage in criminal activity? If so, which groups and why?
- How do you feel about government regulations, such as those related to taxes or environmental protection? Do you believe that these regulations are necessary, or do you see them as unnecessary interference?

It's important to note that not all jurors who express a preference for rules and authority figures necessarily have an authoritarian personality. However, answers to these types of questions can provide insights into a juror's thought process and worldview that may be helpful in identifying potential biases or leanings.

■ CASES IN WHICH YOU MAY WANT AN ANTI-AUTHORITARIAN PERSONALITY

An anti-authoritarian personality is characterized by a skepticism of authority and a willingness to question rules and regulations. Jurors with this type of personality may be particularly well-suited to cases where there is a need to challenge authority, or where the defendant may have acted in ways that were non- conforming or non-traditional.

Some examples include, cases involving alleged violations of civil rights or liberties, an anti-authoritarian personality may be more likely to question the actions of government officials or law enforcement and to prioritize the protection of individual freedoms.

In cases involving protesters or activists who have engaged in civil disobedience, an anti-authoritarian personality may be more likely to understand the motivations behind such actions and to question the validity of laws or regulations that are being protested.

In cases involving alleged violations of drug laws or policies, an anti-authoritarian personality may be more likely to question the efficacy of current drug policies and to consider alternatives to criminalization, such as harm reduction or treatment programs.

In cases involving whistleblowers who have exposed wrongdoing or corruption, an anti-authoritarian personality may be more likely to view the whistle-blower as a heroic figure and to prioritize the protection of those who speak out against authority.

In cases involving alleged violations of free speech or expression, an anti-authoritarian personality may be more likely to prioritize the protection of First Amendment rights and to question the authority of those who seek to suppress speech or expression.

■ VOIR DIRE QUESTIONS TO SPOT AN ANTI-AUTHORITARIAN PERSONALITY

Here are some potential voir dire questions that could help identify jurors who may have an anti-authoritarian personality:

- Do you believe that rules and regulations should always be followed, or are there times when it is appropriate to question or challenge them?
- Have you ever engaged in civil disobedience or protested against authority? If so, what were the circumstances and what motivated you to take such action?
- How do you feel about government officials and institutions? Do you believe that they generally act in the best interest of the public, or do you view them with suspicion or skepticism?
- Do you believe that there are certain groups of people who are unfairly targeted or marginalized by law enforcement or government policies? If so, which groups and why?
- How do you feel about the concept of "whistleblowers" - people who expose wrongdoing or corruption within organizations or institutions? Do you believe that they should be protected, or do you view them as troublemakers?
- Do you believe that the government should have the power to regulate speech and expression, or do you think that individuals should have broad latitude to express themselves as they see fit?

- Have you ever been in a situation where you disagreed with authority figures, such as a boss or teacher? If so, how did you handle the situation?

■ FREE WILL VS. DETERMINISTIC PHILOSOPHIES

In jury selection, free-will personalities can refer to individuals who believe that they have control over their thoughts, emotions, and actions, and that they can make choices based on their own volition. These individuals are likely to value personal responsibility and believe in the importance of individual autonomy.

When selecting a jury, attorneys may look for jurors who possess free-will personalities as they may be more likely to take responsibility for their decisions and be less swayed by external influences. For example, a juror with a free-will personality may be less likely to be influenced by group dynamics or to be intimidated by the opinions of others on the jury.

By contrast, deterministic philosophies refer to the belief that human actions and decisions are determined by factors beyond an individual's control, such as genetics, upbringing, environment, and social conditioning. Individuals who hold deterministic philosophies may believe that free will is an illusion and that people do not have complete control over their thoughts, feelings, and behaviors.

When selecting a jury, attorneys may look for jurors who possess deterministic philosophies as they may be more likely to consider external factors when evaluating evidence and making decisions. For example, a juror with a deterministic philosophy may be more likely to consider the defendant's background and upbringing when evaluating their guilt or innocence.

However, it is important to note that not all deterministic philosophies are the same, and different individuals may have different views on the extent to which determinism affects human behavior. Some individuals may believe that determinism only plays a small role in decision-making, while others may believe that it is the primary factor. As such, attorneys will consider a range of factors when selecting a jury, including the specific case, the judge's instructions, and the demographics of the potential jurors.

It is also important to note that free-will personalities are not the only personality trait that attorneys may look for in jurors. Other personality traits, such as empathy, intelligence, and open-mindedness, may also be important factors in jury selection.

■ CASES IN WHICH YOU MAY WANT A FREE-WILL PERSONALITY

A free-will personality might be particularly useful in cases where personal responsibility is a key issue. For example, in cases where a person has committed a crime, the question of whether they acted of their own free will or were compelled by factors outside of their control is often a critical issue. A free-will personality could help jurors assess whether the defendant acted with full knowledge and control over their actions.

In cases where a person is being sued for damages or negligence, the question of whether they could have acted differently if they had made different choices is often at the heart of the matter. A free-will personality could help jurors determine whether the defendant had the ability to make different choices or was simply following a predetermined course of action.

In cases involving custody battles or disputes over inheritance, the question of personal responsibility and agency is often important. A free-will personality could help jurors assess the intentions and motivations of the parties involved and determine whether they were acting of their own free will.

In general, any case that involves questions of moral responsibility, personal agency, or decision-making would benefit from a juror who believes in free will. Such jurors would be better equipped to assess the motivations and intentions of the parties involved and would be more likely to hold them accountable for their actions.

■ VOIR DIRE QUESTIONS TO SPOT A FREE-WILL PHILOSOPHY

Do you believe that individuals are ultimately responsible for their own actions and decisions? How do you hold yourself accountable for your own decisions?

Do you believe that individuals have the ability to make choices and act independently of external influences? How do you make decisions in your personal and professional life?

Do you believe that individuals have the right to make their own decisions and live their lives according to their own values and beliefs? How do you handle situations where others try to influence or control your decision?

Do you consider yourself to be an independent thinker? How do you ensure that your decisions are duly influenced by others?

What values are most important to you in your personal and professional life? How do these values guide your decision-making process?

■ CASES IN WHICH YOU MAY WANT A DETERMINISTIC PERSONALITY

Deterministic personality traits are characterized by a belief in determinism, which is the idea that all events, including human behavior, are ultimately determined by prior causes, and cannot be altered by free will or choice. Jurors with this type of personality may be particularly well-suited to cases where the behavior of the defendant is believed to be largely determined by factors outside of their control, such as their upbringing, environment, or mental health.

Some examples of cases where a deterministic personality may be beneficial include, cases where the defendant has a diagnosed mental illness, jurors with a deterministic personality may be more likely to view the defendant's actions as being influenced by their mental state and less likely to assign blame or fault to the defendant.

In cases involving addiction, jurors with a deterministic personality may be more likely to understand that the defendant's actions were influenced by their addiction and may be more sympathetic to the challenges of overcoming addiction.

In cases involving child abuse or neglect, jurors with a deterministic personality may be more likely to consider the impact of the defendant's own upbringing and environment on their behavior and may be less likely to view the defendant as solely responsible for their actions.

In cases where the defendant has experienced trauma, jurors with a deterministic personality may be more likely to consider the impact of that trauma on the defendant's behavior and decision-making.

In cases involving environmental pollution or contamination, jurors with a deterministic personality may be more likely to understand the role that environmental factors play in shaping human behavior and may be more sympathetic to the challenges of living in a polluted or contaminated environment.

■ VOIR DIRE QUESTIONS TO SPOT A DETERMINISTIC PERSONALITY

Do you believe that every event in the universe is predetermined and inevitable, or do you think that events happen by chance or free will?

If you believe that everything is predetermined, what is the underlying force or mechanism that determines events?

Do you think that people have complete control over their own lives, or are their actions predetermined by factors such as genetics and the environment?

Is it possible to change the course of events if everything is predetermined, or are all outcomes already set in stone?

What implications does a deterministic philosophy have for concepts such as morality, justice, and personal responsibility?

How does a deterministic philosophy differ from other philosophical viewpoints, such as existentialism or nihilism?

What evidence or arguments support a deterministic worldview, and what evidence or arguments contradict it?

Can a deterministic philosophy coexist with the idea of divine intervention or a higher power guiding event?

How does determinism relate to the scientific concept of causality and the laws of physics?

Do you think that a deterministic philosophy provides a more accurate or complete understanding of the world than other philosophical perspectives?

■ LEADERS VS. FOLLOWERS

In jury selection, identify the "Lions" and the "Lambs." Leader personality traits can be desirable in jury selection because they indicate an ability to take charge and guide others towards a common goal. Leaders are often confident, assertive, and persuasive, and possess excellent communication skills.

When selecting a jury, attorneys may look for jurors who possess leader personality traits as they may be more likely to take charge of group deliberations and guide the jury towards a unanimous decision. A juror with leadership qualities may also be able to effectively communicate with others on the jury and persuade them to see their point of view.

Follower personality traits refer to individuals who are more passive, compliant, and likely to follow the opinions of others in a group setting. These individuals may be less likely to challenge the opinions of others or assert their own views. When selecting a jury, attorneys may look for jurors who possess follower personality traits if they believe that the juror will be easily swayed by their arguments or the arguments of others on the jury.

You want to impanel at least one, but no more than two "lions" on your jury panel and only if they support or believe in your theory of the case. A lion possessing leadership qualities can sway the "lambs" or followers to agree with your position.

■ CASES IN WHICH YOU MAY WANT A LEADER ON YOUR JURY

There are several types of cases in which having a strong leader on the jury could be beneficial. These cases often involve complex or emotionally charged issues, and having a juror with leadership qualities can help to guide the deliberation process and ensure that all perspectives are heard. Some examples of cases where a leader on the jury could be beneficial include, in cases where there are multiple parties involved, a leader on the jury can help to ensure that each party's perspective is heard, and that the deliberation process is organized and efficient.

In cases where scientific or technical evidence is presented, a leader on the jury with expertise in the relevant field can help to guide the discussion and ensure that all jurors have a clear understanding of the evidence. In cases where there is intense media coverage or public interest, a leader on the jury can help to ensure that the deliberation process remains focused and impartial despite external pressures.

In cases where the legal issues are complex or difficult to understand, a leader on the jury with a legal background or experience could help to clarify the issues and ensure that all jurors have a clear understanding of the law.

In cases where emotions are running high, such as in cases involving a victim's family or in cases involving hate crimes or discrimination, a leader on the jury with strong emotional intelligence and empathy can help to ensure that all perspectives are heard, and that the deliberation process is respectful and compassionate.

■ VOIR DIRE QUESTIONS TO SPOT A LEADER PERSONALITY

When conducting voir dire to spot a leader personality, it can be useful to ask questions that assess a potential juror's ability to communicate effectively, listen to others, and take charge when needed. Here are some questions that may help to identify a leader.

- Can you tell us about a time when you had to take charge of a group or lead a project?
- How do you handle conflict or disagreements within a group?
- Have you ever been in a position where you had to make a difficult decision? How did you approach that decision?
- In your opinion, what makes a good leader?
- How do you approach problem-solving within a group?
- Have you ever served on a jury? If so, can you describe your experience?
- How do you feel about speaking up and expressing your opinions in a group setting?
- How do you handle pressure or stress in high- stakes situations?

- Can you describe a time when you had to work with a group of people who had different opinions or perspectives than your own?
- Have you ever had to persuade others to see things from your point of view? How did you go about doing so?

These questions can help to identify potential jurors who have strong leadership qualities and are able to effectively communicate and collaborate with others.

■ CASES IN WHICH YOU MAY WANT A FOLLOWER ON YOUR JURY

While having a leader on a jury can be beneficial in certain cases, having a follower personality on the jury can also be advantageous in certain situations. A follower personality can help to ensure that all jurors are able to participate in the deliberation process and that all perspectives are considered. Here are some examples of cases where a follower on the jury could be beneficial.

In cases where there are strong personalities on the jury or conflicts arise among the jurors, having a follower on the jury can help to diffuse tensions and ensure that all voices are heard.

In cases where the evidence presented is complex or difficult to understand, having a follower on the jury who is willing to listen and follow the guidance of other jurors can help to ensure that all aspects of the evidence are carefully considered.

In cases where the jury is divided or undecided, having a follower on the jury who is willing to listen to the arguments of other jurors and be swayed by persuasive arguments can help to reach a unanimous decision.

In cases where emotional issues are involved, such as cases

involving a victim's family, having a follower on the jury who is empathetic and willing to listen to the emotional perspectives of others can help to ensure that all viewpoints are considered.

When conducting voir dire to identify a potential follower personality, it can be useful to ask questions that assess a potential juror's willingness to listen and follow the guidance of others, as well as their ability to work collaboratively with others. Here are some questions that may help to identify a follower personality.

- How do you approach listening to and considering the opinions of others?
- Have you ever changed your mind about a strongly held belief after hearing the opinions of others? If so, can you describe that experience?
- How do you feel about working collaboratively with others towards a common goal?
- Can you describe a time when you had to work with a group to solve a problem or decide?
- In your opinion, what makes for an effective team or group dynamic?

It is important to note that having a follower personality on the jury does not mean that a juror is incapable of making their own decisions or critically evaluating evidence. Rather, a follower personality is willing to listen to and consider the perspectives of others before making their own decision.

■ PERFECTIONIST PERSONALITIES

In jury selection, perfectionist personalities refer to individuals who have high standards and expectations for themselves and others.

These individuals may be detail-oriented, organized, and motivated to achieve excellence.

When selecting a jury, attorneys may look for jurors who possess perfectionist personalities if attention to detail and careful consideration of evidence is important in the case. For example, in cases involving complex financial transactions or medical procedures, a juror with a perfectionist personality may be more likely to carefully review and analyze the evidence presented.

However, it is important to note that perfectionist personalities may also have drawbacks in jury selection. These individuals may be overly critical, rigid in their thinking, and may struggle with making decisions in the face of uncertainty.

■ CASES IN WHICH YOU MAY WANT A PERFECTIONIST ON YOUR JURY

Having a perfectionist personality on a jury can be beneficial in cases where attention to detail and precision is critical. Some examples of cases where a perfectionist on the jury could be helpful include, in cases where forensic evidence is presented, such as DNA analysis or fingerprint identification, having a perfectionist on the jury who is detail-oriented and meticulous in their evaluation of the evidence can help to ensure that all aspects of the evidence are carefully considered.

In cases where complex financial transactions are involved, such as securities fraud or embezzlement, having a perfectionist on the jury who is able to understand and analyze complex financial data can help to ensure that all aspects of the evidence are carefully considered. In cases where medical malpractice is alleged, having a perfectionist on the jury who is able to carefully evaluate medical records and understand complex medical terminology can help to ensure that all aspects of the evidence are carefully considered.

In cases where construction or engineering defects are alleged, having a perfectionist on the jury who is able to understand technical drawings and evaluate complex engineering data can help to ensure that all aspects of the evidence are carefully considered.

When conducting voir dire to identify a potential perfectionist personality, it can be useful to ask questions that assess a potential juror's attention to detail, ability to analyze complex information, and their willingness to consider all aspects of the evidence. Some questions that may help to identify a perfectionist personality include:

- How do you approach tasks that require attention to detail and precision?
- Can you describe a time when you had to analyze complex information to decide or solve a problem?
- How do you ensure that you consider all aspects of a problem or situation before deciding?
- In your opinion, what makes for a good juror in a complex case?
- Can you describe a time when you had to evaluate technical or scientific data to decide?

It is important to note that while having a perfectionist personality on the jury can be helpful, it is important to ensure that all jurors are able to work collaboratively and consider multiple perspectives in reaching a verdict.

■ NARCISSISTIC PERSONALITIES

In jury selection, narcissistic personalities refer to individuals who have an inflated sense of self-importance, a strong desire for attention and admiration, and a lack of empathy for others. These individuals may believe that they are superior to others and may have difficulty considering the perspectives of others.

When selecting a jury, attorneys may generally seek to avoid jurors who possess narcissistic personalities as they may be more focused on their own opinions and biases, rather than considering the evidence presented. Additionally, they may be more likely to prioritize their own interests over the interests of others on the jury or the defendant.

It is important to note that narcissistic personalities are not always easy to identify during jury selection, as individuals may be able to hide or downplay these traits.

CHAPTER 10

HEURISTICS

■ HEURISTICS AS A FACTOR IN JURY SELECTION

Heuristics refer to mental shortcuts or simplified decision-making strategies that individuals use to make judgments and decisions quickly and efficiently. These heuristics can play a role in jury selection, as attorneys and jury consultants often use various heuristics to assess potential jurors and decide whom to select or strike from the jury pool.

Jurors may also use heuristics or mental shortcuts to make judgments and decisions about the evidence presented during a trial. When trials are complex with conflicting and confusing facts, jurors sometimes use heuristics to help them decide the case. An example of how heuristics can play a role in a juror's decision can be found in a medical malpractice case.

Assume the defendant is a 40-year-old anesthesiologist who

is being sued for professional negligence. Now assume there is a 70-year-old woman juror. During voir dire you learn this juror has a son who is also a doctor. She absolutely adores her son. If the defendant reminds her of her beloved son it is quite possible this juror would be making her decision in this case solely because the defendant reminds her of her son. Other common heuristics that jurors may use to decide cases include:

Anchoring and adjustment heuristic is a cognitive bias in which people use an initial reference point or "anchor" to make subsequent judgments or estimates. The anchor can be a piece of information, a number, or any other stimulus that influences a person's perception of a situation or problem.

Once an anchor is established, people tend to adjust their subsequent judgments or estimates based on the initial anchor, often without sufficient consideration of other relevant information. This can lead to errors in judgment, as people may fail to adjust their estimates enough or may adjust them too much.

For example, if someone is asked to estimate the cost of a new car and is given an initial price of $50,000, they may adjust their estimate up or down from that initial anchor. However, if the actual price of the car is much lower or higher than the initial anchor, their estimate may be biased.

Availability heuristic is a cognitive bias in which people rely on the ease with which they can bring specific examples or instances to mind when making judgments or decisions about a particular topic or event. In other words, people tend to overestimate the likelihood or importance of events that are more easily recalled from memory.

This bias can occur because people tend to assume that the frequency or probability of an event is related to how easily they can remember examples of it. For example, if someone is trying to assess the safety of air travel, they may rely heavily on vivid news stories about plane crashes that they have seen recently, even if such events are rare and statistically unlikely.

The availability heuristic can be useful in some situations, as it allows people to make quick judgments based on information that is easily accessible. However, it can also lead to errors in judgment and decision- making if people do not consider other relevant information or fail to recognize the role that factors such as media coverage or personal experience may play in shaping their perceptions.

Representativeness heuristic is a cognitive bias in which people judge the likelihood of an event or situation based on how well it matches a typical or prototypical example of that category. In other words, people tend to make judgments about something based on how closely it resembles a stereotype or a common mental prototype.

For example, if someone sees a person wearing glasses, carrying books, and walking into a library, they may assume that the person is a librarian, based on their stereotypical image of a librarian. However, this assumption may be incorrect if the person is actually a student, researcher, or someone else who happens to be visiting the library.

The representativeness heuristic can be useful in some situations, as it allows people to quickly make judgments and predictions based on past experience and knowledge. However, it can also lead to errors in judgment and decision-making if people rely too heavily on stereotypes or fail to consider other relevant information.

Illusory correlation involves perceiving a relationship between two variables even when no such relationship exists. Jurors may use this heuristic when drawing conclusions about the defendant's guilt or innocence based on their personal characteristics or behavior.

Hindsight bias, also known as the "I-knew-it-all-along" phenomenon, is a cognitive bias in which people tend to overestimate their ability to have predicted an outcome or event after it has already occurred. In other words, people may believe that an event was more predictable than it actually was, based on their knowledge of the outcome.

This bias can occur because once an outcome is known, people tend to focus on the information that supports their belief that they could have predicted it, while ignoring or downplaying the information that contradicts it. For example, someone might say "I knew all along that the stock market was going to crash," after a market downturn, even if they did not actually predict the specific timing or extent of the crash.

Hindsight bias can be a problem because it can lead to over-confidence in one's ability to predict future events and can make it difficult to learn from mistakes or to identify factors that may have contributed to an unexpected outcome.

Overall, it is important to be aware of hindsight bias and to evaluate events and outcomes based on the information that was available at the time, rather than using knowledge of the outcome to overestimate one's predictive ability. Some common heuristics used by attorneys in jury selection include:

Stereotyping involves making assumptions about individuals based on their demographic characteristics, such as age, gender, race, or occupation. Attorneys may use stereotypes to form judgments about potential jurors' beliefs, attitudes, or experiences, and use this information to decide whether to select or strike them from the jury pool.

Representative bias involves assuming that a sample of individuals selected from a larger population will be representative of that population. Attorneys may use this heuristic to select jurors who they believe will be more representative of the community and more likely to sympathize with their client.

Availability heuristic is a cognitive bias in which people make judgments about the likelihood or frequency of an event based on the ease with which examples or instances of that event come to mind. In other words, people tend to rely on the information that is most easily accessible in memory when making decisions or judgments about the likelihood of an event.

For example, if someone is asked to estimate the frequency of shark attacks in the ocean, they may rely heavily on recent news stories or personal experiences involving shark attacks, even if such events are relatively rare. This can lead them to overestimate the likelihood of such events occurring.

The availability heuristic can be useful in some situations, as it allows people to make quick judgments based on the information that is most easily accessible. However, it can also lead to errors in judgment and decision-making if people do not consider other relevant information or if the information that is most easily accessible is not representative of the overall situation.

Overall, it is important to be aware of the availability heuristic and to try to balance the information that is most easily accessible with other relevant information when making judgments and decisions.

Confirmation bias is a cognitive bias in which people tend to selectively search for, interpret, and remember information in a way that confirms their preexisting beliefs, while ignoring or discounting information that contradicts their beliefs. Attorneys may use this heuristic to focus on information that supports their case and to disregard information that does not.

For example, if someone strongly believes that a certain medical treatment is effective, they may only look for and remember information that supports this belief, while disregarding or downplaying information that suggests otherwise.

It's important to note that heuristics can be useful in certain contexts, but they can also lead to biased or inaccurate decisions if used inappropriately. It's essential that attorneys and jury consultants use multiple sources of information and employ critical thinking skills when selecting jurors to ensure that the jury is fair and impartial.

■ JUROR'S PERCEPTION CAN BE SELECTIVE

Jurors' perceptions can be selective for several reasons, including cognitive biases, personal experiences, and preconceived notions. Cognitive biases are inherent flaws in the way humans process information. For example, confirmation bias is the tendency to seek out information that confirms one's existing beliefs while disregarding information that contradicts them. Jurors may selectively remember or interpret evidence that supports their preconceived notions about a case, while ignoring evidence that challenges those notions.

Personal experiences and background can also influence jurors' perceptions. For example, a juror who has had a negative experience with law enforcement may be more likely to view the police as biased or unreliable witnesses. Similarly, a juror who has been a victim of a crime may be more likely to empathize with the prosecution and view the defendant as guilty.

Finally, preconceived notions and stereotypes can shape jurors' perceptions. For example, a juror may have a stereotype of what a criminal looks like or how they behave and may be more likely to view a defendant who fits that stereotype as guilty. Similarly, a juror may have preconceived notions about the credibility of witnesses based on factors such as their age, race, or profession.

Overall, jurors' perceptions can be influenced by a variety of factors, and it is important for jurors to be aware of their own biases and try to approach the case with an open mind. It is also important for attorneys to carefully select jurors who are likely to be fair and impartial, and to present evidence in a way that is clear and compelling.

Here are a few examples of other heuristics or mental shortcuts attorneys use during jury selection to help them identify potential jurors who are more likely to be sympathetic to their case or more likely to be impartial:

Demographic heuristics: Lawyers may use demographic heuristics, such as age, gender, race, occupation, and education level, to make assumptions about a potential juror's attitudes, beliefs, and values. For instance, a lawyer may assume that a younger juror is more likely to be sympathetic to a defendant, or that an older juror is more likely to be conservative.

Attitudinal heuristics: Lawyers may also use attitudinal heuristics, such as a potential juror's past experiences, beliefs, and opinions, to make judgments about their suitability for a particular case. For instance, a lawyer may ask a potential juror about their views on gun control to gauge their stance on a case involving gun violence.

Group dynamics heuristics: Lawyers may use group dynamics heuristics, such as a potential juror's body language, facial expressions, and interactions with other jurors, to infer their potential biases or sympathies. For example, a lawyer may observe a potential juror's facial expressions during jury selection to gauge their reactions to different questions or arguments.

Stereotyping heuristics: Lawyers may also use stereotyping heuristics, such as assuming that a juror who is a stay-at-home mom is more likely to be sympathetic to the plaintiff, or that a juror who works in law enforcement is more likely to be biased against a defendant.

CHAPTER 11

THE ROLE OF VOIR DIRE

Voir dire is legal process that involves questioning potential jurors to determine their suitability for a particular case. It can be used to expose a schema, which is a pre-existing cognitive structure that shapes how individuals perceive and process new information.

During voir dire, attorneys may ask questions that are designed to elicit jurors' attitudes, beliefs, and biases. These questions can provide insight into the schemas that jurors hold, as well as how those schemas might influence their perceptions of the case.

For example, if a case involves a personal injury claim, attorneys may ask potential jurors about their attitudes towards personal injury lawsuits, their experiences with similar cases, and their beliefs about the responsibility of individuals versus companies for personal injury accidents. These questions can reveal the schemas that jurors hold about personal injury claims, and how those schemas might influence their judgments in the case.

Through voir dire, attorneys can identify potential biases and prejudices that could affect the jurors' decision-making processes. This information can be used to make informed decisions about jury selection and to develop strategies to present evidence and arguments that are most likely to be persuasive to the jurors in the case. By exposing schemas through voir dire, attorneys can better understand how to present their case in a way that resonates with the jurors' existing beliefs and attitudes.

The first and most important thing to do during the voir dire process is understand each juror's "perspective" on the key issue in your case. For example, if the case involves Big Pharma there are some people that have the perspective that the large pharmaceutical companies are evil money grabbers. These people may believe the pharmaceutical companies have the cure for cancer but are keeping it from the rest of us so they can keep making massive profits.

Others believe pharmaceutical companies are angels and they owe their lives and the lives of their families to these selfless behemoth companies. These same people often have the same perspectives on doctors with some having a distrust of doctors and modern medicine and believe only in alternative and minority theories on the cause of disease and proper treatment.

Once a person develops a strong perspective on a particular subject it is difficult or nearly impossible to change their minds. Just think about the political discourse in our country. If you speak to someone who expresses strong right-wing political views and was a devout Donald Trump supporter (assuming those view are contrary to your own believes), some of those individuals continue to believe the 2020 election was rigged, that Donald Trump is still the president years later and hold on to unfounded conspiracy theories. They will hold these views regardless of the evidence you can present to them to the contrary and despite the numerous court rulings debunking that theory. They will deny the validity of the evidence you may provide and only believe what supports their beliefs.

■ USING VOIR DIRE TO DETERMINE JUROR'S FEELING ON LIABILITY

One potential area of inquiry during voir dire is the juror's attitude towards liability.

In order to determine a juror's attitude towards liability, an attorney might ask questions designed to elicit the juror's beliefs about personal responsibility, fault, and negligence. For example, an attorney might ask:

- "Do you believe that individuals should be held accountable for their actions?"
- "In your opinion, what factors should be taken into account when determining fault in a case?"
- "Do you have any biases or prejudices that might influence your ability to fairly assess liability in this case?"

By asking these types of questions, an attorney can gain insight into a potential juror's attitudes and beliefs about liability. This information can be helpful in making informed decisions about which jurors to select for the case.

■ USING VOIR DIRE TO DETERMINE JUROR'S FEELING ON GENERAL DAMAGES

During voir dire, an attorney may also want to e determine a potential juror's attitude towards damages. The attorney may ask questions that are designed to elicit the juror's views on compensation, fairness, and the value of different types of damages. For example, an attorney might ask:

- "Do you believe that people should be compensated for their losses and injuries?"
- "In your opinion, what factors should be taken into account when determining the value of damages in a case?"
- "Do you have any biases or prejudices that might affect your ability to fairly assess damages in this case?"

During voir dire, an attorney may also want to determine a potential juror's attitude towards punitive damages. Punitive damages are awarded in some cases as a way of punishing a defendant for particularly egregious behavior, rather than just compensating the plaintiff for their losses. Punitive damages can be controversial, and some jurors may have strong feelings about when and how they should be awarded.

■ USING VOIR DIRE TO DETERMINE JUROR'S FEELING ON PUNITIVE DAMAGES

To determine a potential juror's attitude towards punitive damages, an attorney may ask questions that are designed to elicit their views on the purpose of punitive damages, the circumstances in which they are appropriate, and the factors that should be considered when determining the amount of punitive damages to award. For example, an attorney might ask:

- "Do you believe that punitive damages serve a valuable purpose in our legal system?"

- "In your opinion, under what circumstances would it be appropriate to award punitive damages?"
- "Do you believe that punitive damages should be limited or capped in some way?"

By asking these types of questions, an attorney can gain insight into a potential juror's attitudes and beliefs about punitive damages. This information can be helpful in making informed decisions about which jurors to select for the case.

However, as with all aspects of voir dire, it's important to approach questioning in a neutral and impartial manner. The goal is to identify jurors who are capable of considering the evidence and making a fair and impartial decision based on the law and the facts of the case. Attorneys should avoid leading questions or attempting to manipulate the selection process in their favor. Ultimately, the goal of voir dire is to select a jury that is fair, impartial, and capable of rendering a just verdict, including any punitive damages that may be appropriate under the law.

■ PEREMPTORY CHALLENGES TO JURORS

A peremptory challenge is a type of challenge that can be used by a party during the jury selection process in a trial. It allows a party to remove a prospective juror from the jury pool without giving a reason or explanation. Each side in a trial may have a limited number of peremptory challenges, which vary depending on the jurisdiction and the type of case.

Peremptory challenges are different from challenges for cause, which are used to remove a prospective juror who has demonstrated a bias or inability to be impartial in the case. Peremptory challenges are often used to remove jurors who a party believes may be unsympathetic to their case or to remove jurors who may be more sympathetic to the other party's case.

Peremptory challenges are subject to some limitations. They cannot be used to remove a juror based on race, gender, or other protected characteristics. Additionally, some jurisdictions have recently limited the use of peremptory challenges in an effort to address concerns about discrimination in jury selection.

■ CHALLENGE FOR CAUSE

When you should use a peremptory challenge becomes a game with your opposing counsel. You usually have half the number of peremptory challenges as you have numbers of jurors. For example, if your jurisdiction requires 12 jurors you get 6 peremptory challenges. If you perceive an unfavorable juror, always try to remove that juror by a challenge for cause. You do not want to waste your peremptory challenges because you have unlimited challenges for cause while your peremptory challenges are limited.

A challenge for cause is a type of challenge that can be made by a party during the jury selection process in a trial. It allows a party to request the removal of a prospective juror from the jury pool for a specific reason or cause, such as a bias or prejudice that would prevent the juror from being fair and impartial in the case.

Challenges for cause are often used to remove jurors who have a relationship with one of the parties or witnesses, who have preconceived opinions about the case, or the parties involved, or who may be unable to be fair and impartial due to their personal beliefs or experiences.

The party making the challenge for cause must provide a specific reason or evidence to support the challenge. The judge will then decide whether to grant the challenge and remove the juror from the jury pool.

Unlike peremptory challenges, there is no limit on the number of challenges for a cause that a party can make. However, the party must provide a valid reason for each challenge and the judge must agree that there is sufficient cause to remove the juror from the jury pool.

One strategy in using your peremptory challenges is to accept the panel as constituted even though there may be one or two more jurors you would exclude if you had more challenges. This way your opposing party would exercise one of his or her challenges. Once your opponent runs out of challenges you have complete control over the jury panel. The risk is your opposing counsel may also accept the panel as constituted and you may be struck with some unfavorable jurors.

During voir dire, attorneys have the opportunity to identify potential jurors who may be biased, prejudiced, or otherwise unsuitable for the case. If an attorney believes that a potential juror cannot be impartial or fair, they may ask the court to excuse that juror "for cause." Here are some possible voir dire questions that an attorney might use to identify potential jurors who could be excused for cause:

- "Have you or someone close to you ever been involved in a similar case, or one that is related to this case?"
- "Do you have any preconceived notions or biases that could affect your ability to be impartial in this case?"
- "Have you ever expressed an opinion or made a statement about this case or a similar case?" "Do you have any personal or professional relationships with anyone involved in this case?"
- "Do you have any personal beliefs or experiences that might prevent you from being able to follow the law and make a fair and impartial decision?"

If a potential juror answers "yes" to any of these questions or otherwise raises concerns about their ability to be impartial, the attorney may ask follow-up questions or request that the juror be excused for cause. It's important to note that the decision to excuse a juror for cause ultimately rests with the judge, who will consider the specific circumstances of the case and the juror's responses during voir dire.

■ VOIR DIRE QUESTIONS TO UNCOVER DIFFERENT PERSONALITY TRAITS

Here are some sample voir dire questions that may help uncover different personality traits:

Openness:

- "Do you consider yourself to be open-minded and willing to consider different perspectives?"
- "Can you tell me about a time when you changed your mind about a strongly held belief?"

Conscientiousness:

- "How do you prioritize your responsibilities and manage your time?"
- "Are you someone who always follows through on your commitments?"

Emotional stability:

- "Can you describe a situation that caused you significant stress, and how did you cope with it?"
- "Are you someone who is easily upset or stressed out?"

Agreeableness:

- "How do you approach conflicts or disagreements with others?"
- "Can you give me an example of a time when you had to compromise to reach a solution?"

Extraversion:

- "Do you enjoy meeting new people and socializing?"
- "Are you comfortable speaking up and sharing your opinions in group settings?"

■ LAWSUITS

- Do you know anyone who has been sued?
- Do you feel there are too many lawsuits filed?
- How do you feel about the number of lawsuits that are being filed?
- Do you feel there are a lot of frivolous lawsuits? Anybody know anybody who has been accused of selling a counterfeit product?
- What sort of proof would you want to hear to decide if someone accused of selling a counterfeit product actually sold a counterfeit product?
- If someone accused another of being a counterfeiter how certain should they be that the person accused is actually a counterfeiter? That is a serious accusation. Because of the seriousness does that mean the accuser should have strong evidence
- Has anybody heard about something called "Tort reform"? It is legislation that restricts the number of lawsuits.

- Who is in favor of tort reform?
- Do you think that before someone files a lawsuit that need to make sure the party they are suing actually did something wrong and deserved to be sued?
- Do you think jury verdicts are too high? Should there be a limit on the amount of money someone can recover when filing a lawsuit?

You will hear the plaintiff's lawyer go first and tell you about this lawsuit. There are two sides to every story.

■ GENERAL QUESTIONS IN VOIR DIRE

1. Do you know anybody who owns a small business?
2. What type of jobs have you primarily held?
3. Level of education?
4. Subjects you did well at in college?
5. Subjects you did not like?
6. Stronger in math and science or prefer English literature?

You can use heuristics to spot a cognitive personality by asking if anyone held a position as:

Carpenter
Electricians
Mechanic MBA
Accountant

- Do you consider yourself politically conservative or more liberal as a heuristics to spot an authoritarian or anti-authoritarian personality?

- Ever serve in the military or have friends and family members that served?
- How do you feel about people who served in the military?
- Does anybody have any friends or family members who work in law enforcement? How do you feel about law and order?
- Are we too lax in this country on law and order?
- How could things be different?
- How do you feel about people who say we should de-fund the police?
- How about de-funding the FBI and other law enforcement?

Exposing a prospective juror's views that conflict with your theory of the case is the single most important aspect of the voir dire process.

■ ANCHOR THE TAG LINE INTO YOUR VOIR DIRE QUESTIONS

As you can see you can start to anchor your "tag line" during the voir dire process. If a tag line is "We didn't know" referring to the fact the defendant merely bought genuine goods and resold them without knowing they were counterfeit, you can anchor that phrase into your voir dire questions.

■ SAMPLE VOIR DIRE QUESTIONS IN A BREACH OF CONTRACT CASE

Voir dire is the process of questioning potential jurors to determine if they are qualified to serve on a jury. In a breach of contract case, here are some sample voir dire questions that the attorneys may ask:

- Have you ever been involved in a breach of contract dispute before, either as a party or a witness?

- Do you know anyone who works in the same industry as the defendant?
- Have you ever had a contract dispute with someone, whether it was resolved in court or not?
- Do you have any personal beliefs or experiences that would prevent you from being fair and impartial in this case?
- Have you ever had a negative experience with a business or contract that would make it difficult for you to remain unbiased in this case?
- Are you aware of any biases or prejudices that could impact your ability to be fair and impartial in this case?
- Do you have any preconceived notions about breach of contract cases that would prevent you from objectively evaluating the evidence presented in court?
- Have you ever been a party to a contract that was breached, and if so, how did you handle the situation?
- Do you have any financial or personal connections to the parties involved in this case?
- Are you comfortable evaluating the evidence and deciding based solely on the facts presented in court, without being influenced by outside factors or opinions?

■ SAMPLE VOIR DIRE QUESTIONS IN A NEGLIGENCE CASE

In a negligence case, the attorneys may ask the following sample voir dire questions to potential jurors:

- Have you ever been involved in a personal injury case, either as a party or a witness?
- Do you have any medical or legal training that could impact your ability to be fair and impartial in this case?

- Have you ever been in an accident, and if so, how did you handle the situation?
- Do you know anyone who works in the same industry as the defendant or plaintiff?
- Are you aware of any biases or prejudices that could impact your ability to be fair and impartial in this case?
- Have you ever formed an opinion about personal injury lawsuits or the civil justice system that would make it difficult for you to be fair and impartial in this case?
- Have you or anyone you know ever filed a personal injury lawsuit, and if so, what was the outcome?
- Are you comfortable evaluating the evidence and deciding based solely on the facts presented in court, without being influenced by outside factors or opinions?
- Have you ever been a party to a contract or agreement that included a waiver of liability or assumption of risk clause?
- Have you ever had a negative experience with a business or industry related to this case that would make it difficult for you to remain unbiased?

■ SAMPLE VOIR DIRE QUESTIONS IN A TRADE SECRETS CASE

In a trade secrets case, the attorneys may ask the following sample voir dire questions to potential jurors:

- Have you ever worked in a company that dealt with trade secrets or confidential information?
- Do you have any experience with the industry in which the defendant and plaintiff operate?

- Have you ever signed a confidentiality or non-disclosure agreement?
- Do you know anyone who works in the same industry as the defendant or plaintiff?
- Have you ever been involved in a dispute over confidential information or trade secrets?
- Are you aware of any biases or prejudices that could impact your ability to be fair and impartial in this case?
- Have you ever formed an opinion about trade secret disputes or the civil justice system that would make it difficult for you to be fair and impartial in this case?
- Are you comfortable evaluating the evidence and deciding based solely on the facts presented in court, without being influenced by outside factors or opinions?
- Have you ever worked for a competitor of the plaintiff or defendant?
- Have you ever been sued for misappropriation of trade secrets or intellectual property infringement, and if so, what was the outcome?

■ SAMPLE VOIR DIRE QUESTIONS IN AN INTERFERENCE WITH ECONOMIC RELATIONS CASE

In an interference with economic relations case, the attorneys may ask the following sample voir dire questions to potential jurors:

- Have you ever been involved in a dispute over business relationships or contracts?
- Do you have any experience with the industry in which the plaintiff and defendant operate?

- Have you ever worked for or with the plaintiff or defendant, or a competitor of either party? Do you know anyone who works in the same industry as the plaintiff or defendant?
- Are you aware of any biases or prejudices that could impact your ability to be fair and impartial in this case?
- Have you ever formed an opinion about interference with economic relations or the civil justice system that would make it difficult for you to be fair and impartial in this case?
- Have you ever been in a business relationship that was interfered with by a third party, and if so, how did you handle the situation?
- Are you comfortable evaluating the evidence and deciding based solely on the facts presented in court, without being influenced by outside factors or opinions?
- Have you ever had a negative experience with a business or industry related to this case that would make it difficult for you to remain unbiased?
- Have you ever been sued for interference with economic relations or tortious interference, and if so, what was the outcome?

■ SAMPLE VOIR DIRE QUESTIONS IN A FRAUD CASE

In a fraud case, the attorneys may ask the following sample voir dire questions to potential jurors:

- Have you ever been involved in a case that involved allegations of fraud or misrepresentation, either as a party or a witness?
- Do you have any experience with the industry in which the defendant or plaintiff operates?
- Have you ever been a victim of fraud or misrepresentation?

- Do you know anyone who works in the same industry as the defendant or plaintiff?
- Are you aware of any biases or prejudices that could impact your ability to be fair and impartial in this case?
- Have you ever formed an opinion about fraud cases or the civil justice system that would make it difficult for you to be fair and impartial in this case?
- Have you ever been involved in a business transaction that involved misrepresentation or fraudulent activity?
- Are you comfortable evaluating the evidence and deciding based solely on the facts presented in court, without being influenced by outside factors or opinions?
- Have you ever had a negative experience with a business or industry related to this case that would make it difficult for you to remain unbiased?
- Have you ever been sued for fraud or accused of fraudulent activity, and if so, what was the outcome?
- Have you ever heard the expression "no good deed goes unpunished?"
- What does that mean?
- Does that apply in this case?

■ IDENTIFYING JUROR'S ATTITUDE ON TORT REFORM

Tort reform refers to changes in the legal system that aim to limit the amount of damages that can be awarded in personal injury cases. This is a controversial issue, and jurors may have different views on the subject.

Here are some possible voir dire questions that an attorney might use to identify potential jurors' attitudes towards tort reform:

- "Have you ever heard of tort reform?"
- What is your understanding of the concept?" "Do you have any personal beliefs or opinions about tort reform?"
- "Do you believe that there are situations where it is appropriate to award large damages in personal injury cases?"
- "Do you believe that the legal system should be reformed to limit the amount of damages that can be awarded in personal injury cases?"

By asking these types of questions, an attorney can gain insight into a potential juror's attitudes and beliefs about tort reform. This information can be helpful in making informed decisions about which jurors to select for the case. However, it's important to approach questioning in a neutral and impartial manner.

■ COVER THE "SCHEMA" THEORY AND THE PERSONALITY TRAIT THEORY IN JURY SELECTION

Use voir dire questions to focus on the juror's "perspective" or "schema." In questioning in this manner always ask "how do you feel" about a topic. You are trying to get an emotional response. You also need to add voir dire questions on individual personality traits.

In federal court depending on the circuit the judges conduct the voir dire and do not allow the attorneys to ask questions. Instead, they encourage the attorneys to propose voir dire questions to the judge who then decides which questions to ask during voir dire. When this happens, the attorneys have to rely upon their heuristics or shortcuts in selecting or removing a juror.

For example, if the case involves a trademark infringement and there are issues that are highly technical and other issues that require the jurors to consider more of the human elements, you may want some jurors who have a cognitive personality trait to deal with the technical issues and some jurors with an affective personality trait to address the emotional issues.

If you want a cognitive personality in your jury and know that cognitive personalities are found in professions like science, engineering, technology, research, finance, accounting, or medicine the attorney may make his decision based on the job or profession of the prospective juror.

If you want an affective personality in your jury and know that affective personalities are found in professions like teaching, counseling, performing arts, entertainment, nursing or health care or human resources, the attorney will use the same heuristic in making his or her decision.

CHAPTER 12

USING PATHOS TO PERSUADE A JURY

The art of persuasive communication involves the use of ethos, pathos, and logos to appeal to an audience. These three persuasive appeals are crucial in jury selection, where attorneys seek to select jurors who will be most likely to empathize with their client's position and deliver a favorable verdict.

Ethos refers to the credibility and trustworthiness of the speaker or argument. In jury selection, attorneys use ethos to establish their own credibility and expertise and to build trust with potential jurors. Attorneys may present their qualifications, experience, and legal victories to establish their ethos and persuade potential jurors to trust them and their arguments.

Pathos appeals to the emotions of the audience. In jury selection, attorneys use pathos to connect with potential jurors on a personal level, appealing to their emotions and values. Attorneys may use personal anecdotes, powerful stories, and vivid descriptions to evoke emotions and build a sense of empathy between potential jurors and their clients.

Logos refers to the logical and rational appeal of an argument. In jury selection, attorneys use logos to present a compelling and persuasive case that is grounded in facts and evidence. Attorneys may use statistics, expert testimony, and logical reasoning to build a strong argument that is both convincing and compelling to potential jurors.

The use of ethos, pathos, and logos is crucial in jury selection. By establishing their credibility and expertise, appealing to the emotions of potential jurors, and presenting a compelling and persuasive case grounded in facts and evidence, attorneys can select jurors who are most likely to empathize with their client's position and deliver a favorable verdict.

Pathos is a rhetorical technique that legal scholars suggest the best opening statement tell a captivating story to the jurors. People are wired to respond to stories, and a well-crafted story can be very persuasive. Use storytelling techniques to create a narrative that engages the jury's emotions and draws them into the case.

The best way to learn how to tell a compelling story is by reading classic literature and see the masters in their glory to persuade an audience. It can be effective in persuading a jury by connecting with them on a personal and emotional level.

Here are some ways that pathos can be used to persuade a jury:

Tell a story: Humans are wired to respond to stories, and a well-crafted story can be very persuasive. Use storytelling techniques to create a narrative that engages the jury's emotions and draws them into the case.

Use vivid language: Use descriptive and evocative language to create powerful images in the minds of the jurors. This can help them to connect with the emotional content of the case.

Use analogies and metaphors: Analogies and metaphors can be powerful tools for persuasion, as they can help to explain complex ideas in a way that is easy to understand and emotionally resonant.

Appeal to shared values: Identify the values that the jurors hold dear and connect the case to those values. For example, if the case involves a victim of a crime, appeal to the jurors' sense of justice and fairness.

Use personal anecdotes: Sharing personal stories and experiences can be a powerful way to connect with jurors on an emotional level. This can help to build trust and credibility with the jury.

It's important to note that while pathos can be a powerful tool for persuasion, it should be used ethically and responsibly. Any attempts to manipulate or exploit the emotions of the jury can be perceived as insincere and can backfire.

■ ESTABLISHING RAPPORT WITH THE JURY

Establishing rapport with the jury is crucial for a lawyer to build trust, credibility, and to create a positive impression that can affect the outcome of the case. To establish rapport with the jury start by introducing yourself and expressing gratitude for the jury's service. Make eye contact with the jurors and use their names when addressing them.

It is important to be genuine and humble. Jurors can easily sense if a lawyer is being insincere or fake. Be authentic and sincere in your communication with the jury.

When you ask a prospective juror a question, make sure you listen to their answer and keep eye contact. I have seen lawyers during voir dire ask a question to a juror and then keep looking at their notes to see their next question or spend time writing the juror's answer. It is important to show respect to the jurors by listening to their questions and opinions. Avoid interrupting or talking down to them. Instead of taking notes while engaging in voir dire, delegate that task to a co-counsel or trial consultant.

Every second when you are in front of a jury, at least one juror is looking at you and studying your behavior. It is imperative you make a good first impression. The way you make a good first impression is if you look like a competent and organized professional attorney. The first things juror's see is how you are dressed and the physical impression you make. Wear a good quality suit that displays the current fashion and is properly tailored. When you walk into the courtroom you do not want people to notice your clothes, you want them to notice you. Avoid trendy clothes and ostentatious jewelry. Your clothes should be classic and elegant. Proper grooming is equally important. Make sure your hair is styled and your fingernails are clipped and clean.

We can establish credibility by the way we carry ourselves and through our non-verbal communication. We all emit non-verbal cues that can influence a jury. The colors you wear can affect how others perceive you and can communicate non-verbally. Different colors can evoke different emotions and convey different meanings, and these can impact how others view your credibility.

Earth tones such as brown, beige, and green can be a good choice for a lawyer's outfit during their opening statement as they suggest stability, reliability, and harmony. These colors are also considered natural and calming, which can be useful in creating a positive first impression on the jury and the judge.

Wearing dark or neutral colors are often associated with business settings and can help create a sense of seriousness and responsibility. Gray is a professional color that suggests sophistication, neutrality, and balance. It can be a good choice for a lawyer's outfit, especially if combined with other colors such as navy blue or black.

Black is a powerful color that signifies formality, seriousness, and professionalism. It's an excellent choice for a lawyer's outfit, especially for a courtroom appearance while white is a pure, clean color that suggests professionalism, sincerity, and integrity.

Burgundy is a rich, warm color that conveys elegance, sophistication, and authority. It can be a good choice for a lawyer's outfit, especially for a courtroom appearance.

You may want to wait until you are engaged in the cross examination of your opponent's key witness before you pull out the navy-blue suit, white shirt, and red tie. Navy blue is a classic color that conveys authority, confidence, and credibility. Pairing the navy-blue suit with a white shirt and red tie signifies that a lawyer is ready to get tough and relentless in his or her examination. It fits in with what most people expect to see when witnessing a trial.

Avoid using legal jargon or technical terms that jurors may not understand. Use plain language to make your points clear and easy to understand. Be confident and prepared. Jurors will be more likely to trust a lawyer who appears confident and well-prepared. Make sure you are well-prepared for your case and present your arguments with confidence.

Make sure your counsel table is organized and free of clutter. Keep your case binders for trial in notebooks or banker boxes. Your goal is to be able to find any piece of evidence within 15 seconds. If you stumble on finding a document, you lose credibility.

You always want to appear you are in control or your case and that you are reliable and trustworthy. Always show respect for your opposing counsel, all the parties including your opponent's client and witnesses, the judge, the court's clerk and its entire and its staff. Don't "beat up" or try to destroy a witness on cross examination. Jurors do not like a lawyer who belittles or is disrespectful to a witness. Your goal in cross examination is get to the truth, not humiliate a witness.

I tried a case where I represented a party suing a landscape architect for breach of contract and professional negligence. I felt some compassion for her and did not think she was a bad person. During my cross examination I called her by her first name and showed her respect. I wasn't doing that to gain sympathy with the jury, which is the way I actually felt. After the trial one juror came up to me and said she liked the way I treated my opposing party. I was a little surprised, but I learned a lesson. The lesson I learned is that you risk your case if you come off as being a bully or being unfair.

People in general appreciate people who treat others kindly and with respect. Remember, the key to establishing rapport with the jury is to be personable, respectful, and relatable. By creating a positive connection with the jury, a lawyer can increase their chances of winning the case.

■ USE THE MIRRORING TECHNIQUE TO ESTABLISH RAPPORT

Mirroring is a technique used to establish rapport with others by reflecting their nonverbal behavior back to them. It involves mimicking the posture, gestures, and facial expressions of the person with whom you are communicating.

To establish rapport with the jury the lawyer needs to pay close attention to the body language and nonverbal cues of the jurors. Notice their posture, hand gestures, facial expressions, and tone of voice.

Once you have observed the jurors' nonverbal behavior, subtly mirror their body language and gestures. For example, if a juror is leaning forward and nodding their head, you can do the same. It's important to be subtle when mirroring the jury's behavior. If you overdo it, it may come across as insincere or manipulative.

Once you have established a connection with the jurors through mirroring, you can use pacing and leading to guide the conversation. Pacing involves matching the jury's behavior, while leading involves gradually changing your behavior to lead the conversation in a particular direction.

During voir dire you want to keep the jurors talking. The best way to accomplish that is by repeating back the last three of the juror's own words. This powerfully shows the juror you really do understand her and are not just merely parroting her concerns the juror will usually continue expanding on what they previously said.

For example, if you ask a juror how they feel about the debate in Congress over gun control, the juror may respond by saying: "The representatives in Congress seem too busy to deal with the problem." You repeat the juror's last words by saying: "deal with the problem" in a tone that shows you heard what she said and are curious about her response. The juror may then say: "Yeah. There is a serious problem in this country where people are being shot and nobody seems to care." This way you showed the juror you care about her feelings and by getting her to speak further on this topic you learned more about some of her personality traits.

Overall, mirroring can be an effective technique for establishing rapport with the jury. By matching their nonverbal behavior, a lawyer can create a sense of familiarity and trust with the jury.

CHAPTER 13

CONDITIONING THE JURY

During a trial, the judge frequently instructs the jury to reserve any decisions about this case until they hear all the evidence and are involved in their deliberations. Despite this admonition, there is evidence that most jurors are influenced and form an initial opinion in the outcome of the case early in the trial.

Research suggests that many jurors form preliminary opinions of a case based on opening statements. Opening statements are an important part of a trial because they provide the first opportunity for each side to present its version of events and to outline the evidence that will be presented. Jurors may form opinions about the credibility of the attorneys, witnesses, and evidence based on these initial presentations.

Some studies have found that as many as 80-90% of jurors form preliminary opinions about a case during opening statements. These opinions may change as the trial progresses and more evidence is presented. However, once someone forms an opinion it can be difficult to get them to change their mind. In order to get someone to change their mind, they have to admit they made a mistake. Some people have difficulty admitting they made a mistake.

It's also worth noting that some jurors may be more influenced by opening statements than others, depending on factors such as their prior experiences, attitudes, and biases. Ultimately, it's important for attorneys to carefully consider their approach to opening statements and to strive to present their case in a way that is both persuasive and fair. By doing so, they can help ensure that jurors are able to make informed and impartial decisions based on the evidence presented at trial.

You condition the jury by repeating your theory of the case and your tagline at every phase of the trial. During voir dire you can tell the jury what the case is about by reciting a version of your theory of the case. When telling your theory of the case you tell the jury your tagline as the summary or the essence of your theory of the case.

During your opening statement you have another opportunity to tell the jury your theory of the case and your tag line. Look for any opportunity to state your tagline once again to the jury during your direct or cross examination of any witness. In your closing argument you repeat your tagline for the last time. By repeating your tag line throughout the trial, you are conditioning the jury so during their deliberations you hope the jury will repeat your tag line in rendering a favorable verdict for your client.

Here is a little test to show the effect of conditioning. Ask a friend to answer a series of questions that are provided in a rapid-fire succession.

1. What is the color of the shirt I am wearing? White
2. What is the color of this piece of paper? White

3. What is the color of snow? White
4. What do cows drink? Milk

The person was conditioned to answer the last question by saying "Milk" when cows do not drink milk; they drink water. The person answered milk because they were conditioned to think of everything white. This type of conditioning can happen when you anchor your tag line throughout the case to condition the jurors.

CHAPTER 14

CREATING YOUR CASE SUMMARY

reating an outline of the issues in the case should start early in the litigation and be constantly updated. What follows is a summary I prepared in a very contentious business litigation case. I changed the names and deleted portions of the document to protect my client's confidentiality. This is a work in progress which evolves throughout the litigation process.

■ MEMORANDUM

Theory of the Case

Smith entered into a joint venture partnership with Jones and Cain to co-own, co-manage and share profits on a digital streaming company. Smith paid Jones several million for the first-year budget to be used exclusively to create the necessary technology. Within that year Jones spent only a fraction of that money and repudiated the contract claiming it was incapable of fulfilling the contract. Instead of returning what was not yet spent, Jones kept Smith's money.

Triggering Event

An April 14, 2018, email from Jones stating that within the last 12 months Jones was already phasing out content and will only do technology. Smith needed to find somebody else to do content, marketing, and distribution. Jones repudiated 97% of the contract.

Theme/Tag Line (s)

Don't promise what you can't perform. Without trust you cannot have a relationship. Some people can't be trusted.

No good deed goes unpunished.

Juror Profile

I think our ideal juror would be: (a) a cognitive as opposed to an affective personality. MBA, majored in business, math, accounting, bookkeeping, physical science. Jobs like electricians, mechanics, carpenters. Intellectually controlled. (b) authoritarian personality. Regards people in authority like law enforcement, judges, military. Politically conservative, intolerant, punitive, close minded. Dresses up for jury service. Men may wear tie and jacket.

Smith Claims

Smith filed suit against Jones. Smith' operative pleading is its Second Amended Complaint. The primary legal theories are breach of contract, fraud, conversion, and claim and delivery (common law replevin) to reclaim the domain name and source code transferred back to Smith.

Breach of Contract

A cause of action for breach of contract requires proof of the following elements: (1) existence of the contract; (2) the plaintiff's performance or excuse for nonperformance; (3) the defendant's breach; and (4) damages to the plaintiff as a result of the breach.

Fraud

The elements of fraud are (1) the defendant made a false representation as to a past or existing material fact; (2) the defendant knew the representation was false at the time it was made; (3) in making the representation, the defendant intended to deceive the plaintiff; (4) the plaintiff justifiably relied on the representation; and (5) the plaintiff suffered resulting damages.

Promissory fraud is a promise made without any intention of performing it. The fraud exception to the parol evidence rule does not apply to such promissory fraud if the evidence in question is offered to show a promise which contradicts an integrated written agreement. Unless the false promise is either independent of or consistent with the written instrument, evidence thereof is inadmissible.

Conversion

Conversion is the wrongful exercise or command over the property of another. (Farmers Ins. Exchange v. Zerin (1997) 53 Cal.App.4th 445, 451, 61 Cal. Rptr. 2d 707.) The elements of a conversion actions are: (1) the plaintiff's ownership or right to possession of the property at the time of conversion; (2) the defendant's conversion by a wrongful act or disposition of the property rights; and (3) damages.

Replevin

In an action in replevin or claim and delivery, being an action for the recovery of specific personal property, in order to sustain a judgment for the plaintiff, it must be shown that possession was in the defendant at the time of the beginning of the action or that he had the power to make delivery of the personal property for the recovery of which the action is prosecuted. We want possession of all the content that we paid to Jones.

Jones Claims

Jones has a variety of claims. We have raised several affirmative defenses including the following affirmative defenses:

Litigation Strategy

We will put our case on by relying on our documents. Smith's amended and restated operating agreement provides strong support that all of Smith's actions were authorized by a written operating agreement signed by the members of Smith.

Risks and Rewards

We have an 80% chance of prevailing on our breach of contract claim. We have a 50% chance of receiving a punitive damage award, and a 50% chance of being awarded $10 million in lost profits. The contract has an attorney fees provision. Our motion for attorney fees as the prevailing parties should be around $400-$500,000. I predict

Jones has a 15% prevailing on their cross complaint. It is not possible to predict with certainty any jury verdict; however we are on the better side of this case, and I think our side will come off as a more sympathetic and credible party.

Collectability

Jones collected millions of dollars from its securities offerings that were the subject of a prior governmental action.

CHAPTER 15

KEEPING TRACK OF KEY DOCUMENTS

Organizing and cataloging documents obtained in discovery is an essential part of preparing for trial. Here are some steps you can follow to effectively manage the documents:

Review and assess the documents: Carefully review each document obtained in discovery to determine its relevance to the case. You should also evaluate the document's potential value as evidence and identify any privileged or confidential information.

Create a document database: A document database is a centralized location to store and organize all the documents related to the case. There are various tools available for creating a document database, including commercial software and online document management systems. You should choose the one that best suits your needs.

Categorize the documents: Divide the documents into categories, such as witness statements, expert reports, and medical records. You can also create sub-categories within each category, such as chronological order, relevance, or type of document.

Index the documents: Indexing involves assigning unique identifying numbers to each document to facilitate quick and easy retrieval. You can use document management software to automate the indexing process.

Create a document log: A document log is a record of all the documents obtained in discovery, including the date they were received, the source, and the status. It is essential to maintain an accurate document log to ensure that all documents are accounted for and to avoid the risk of losing any crucial evidence.

Maintain confidentiality: Ensure that confidential or privileged documents are kept secure and are not accessible to unauthorized persons.

In complex litigation cases it is common to feel overwhelmed with massive amounts of documents. It is important to be able to create a system quickly and efficiently where you can locate key documents. One system I prefer is as follows:

1. Scan all your client's documents and the documents you receive in discovery and place those documents on your computer hard drive.

2. Bates number these documents and combine all the documents in a single pdf. File.

3. Using an Optical Character Recognition (OCR) software feature makes all the documents searchable.

4. Create a log where you list the documents by bates number, type of document, author of the document, recipient of the document, brief description of the document using key works, the issue in the case and whether the document is a key document to be used at trial. It looks like this:

Bates	Author	Recipient	Document	Issue	Key
001-002	Smith	Jones; Cain	email	contract formation	
003-025	Jones	McDuffy	contract	breach	Key
026-125	Wilson		deposition	admissions	Key
126-130	Smith	Jones	letter	mitigation	

Once you have reviewed each document and listed each document in your log, you can search your documents by entering any searchable term. If you want to take the deposition of Jones and need to review documents to prepare for that deposition, merely type Control F followed by "Jones" and you will see each document where Jones' name appears. If you want to see a list of all your key documents merely hit Control F followed by "Key" and you will immediately get a list of all the key documents for your trial.

■ MAKING YOUR EXHIBIT LIST MANAGEABLE

The courts require all parties to submit a joint exhibit list at the final status conference before trial. When you are in trial sometimes you need to find a particular document which can be difficult if you have a lot of exhibits. The goal in a trial is to be able to put your finger on any document or piece of evidence in 15 seconds. One way is to add an extra column to your exhibit list with a short description of each document. This is *your* exhibit list and not the exhibit list submitted to the court jointly prepared with your opposing counsel.

Exhibit	Description	Comment
1	Notice of Bidder-Bid package	plaintiff's scope of contract
2	Addendum No. 2	condition of site
3	Agreement of Indemnity	Indemnity
4	Addendum 5-August 5, 2010	Bid package 24
5	Contract dated August 19, 2010	Contract bid 26
6	Notice to Proceed dated September 13, 2010	
7	Performance bond	bond
8	Owner's change order	Change order
9	Submittal	Change order
10	Summary of Change orders-item 16 seal conduits	Change order
11	Completed punch list-final walk through September 6, 2011	Performance
12	Letter to Bank-Notice of completion July 11, 2012	Completion of contract
13	Attorney letter dated July 25, 2012	Claim of breach
14	Settlement Agreement on prior case	Mitigate-**KEY**
15	Attorney letter dated August 19, 2015, letter re: defects on project	Defects
16	Lawsuit filed	Joint liability **KEY**
17	Defects Report	Owner's claim
18	Complaint in federal court	
19	Settlement Agreement	Contract-**KEY**

CHAPTER 16

THE ART OF WAR

magine Tai Tzu is a young general looking to engage with a nomadic tribe of Wu Hu warriors in battle. Tai Tzu knew the Wu Hu were skilled horsemen and archers, and their hit-and-run tactics could be difficult to counter. Unsure how to defend against these skilled warriors Tai Tzu needed a strategy to gain an advantage against this superior rival.

Tai Tzu felt one way to defend against them would be to fortify defensive positions such as walls, gates, or cities. This would force Wu Hu to engage in direct combat, which would negate their mobility advantage.

Another tactic to defeat Wu Hu warriors would be to use traps and ambushes. The Wu Hu were known for their speed and mobility, so creating obstacles in their path, such as pits, ditches, or traps, would slow them down and make them easier to target. Ambushes could also be set up in areas where the Wu Hu were likely to pass through.

To counter Wu Hu's proficiency in archery, an army facing them could also deploy their own skilled archers. Archers could take up positions on high ground or behind cover and rain arrows down on the Wu Hu, forcing them to keep their distance or risk being picked off.

The struggles Tai Tzu faced in the fifth century are reminiscent of what a young attorney faces in modern day litigation. Lessons can be learned by reading a book written by Sun Tzu called The Art of War.

The Art of War is a classic Chinese military treatise written by Sun Tzu during the 5th century BC. The book is a comprehensive guide to military strategy and tactics, covering everything from battlefield tactics to political maneuvering. The strategies outlined in The Art of War are still studied and applied by military leaders and businesspeople today.

Sun Tzu emphasized the importance of understanding both yourself and your opponent. A commander should know their own strengths and weaknesses, as well as those of their enemy. This understanding can help them develop effective strategies and tactics.

He believed that deception was a powerful tool in warfare. He encouraged commanders to mislead their opponents and make them believe that they were weak or strong when they were not. This could be achieved through the use of spies, false information, and feints. Sun Tzu advised commanders to identify and attack the weakest points in their enemy's defenses. This could be done by studying the terrain, the enemy's troop movements, and their supply lines.

He believed that speed and surprise could be used to gain an advantage over an opponent. He advised commanders to move quickly and attack unexpectedly to catch their enemy off guard. And Sun

Tzu believed that a successful commander must be able to adapt to changing circumstances. They should be flexible and able to adjust their strategies and tactics as the situation evolves.

According to Sun Tzu the best way to win a battle was to avoid it altogether. He advised commanders to only engage in battle when they were certain of victory and to avoid battles that were likely to result in defeat.

The Art of War emphasizes the importance of careful planning, strategic thinking, and adaptability in warfare. By following these strategies, a commander can gain a significant advantage over their opponent and achieve victory. With careful thought these same strategies can be modified and used to your advantage in modern litigation.

CHAPTER 17

MOTIONS IN LIMINE

One especially important aspect when engaging in complex business litigation and trial work is having certain issues decided by the court before the trial begins, outside the presence of a jury. This is done by something called a motion *in limine,* a Latin term meaning *at the doorstep,* so it is an issue that is raised at the doorstep, before the trial begins.

This usually relates to a claim by one party to exclude certain evidence that they expect the other side will try to introduce. The position for wanting to exclude the evidence would be that it was either irrelevant, it would result in an undue consumption of time, or that it would be unduly prejudicial. These motions allow the court to carefully consider this, outside the heat of battle at trial.

Another reason to use a motion in limine is if there is certain evidence that you want to have introduced at trial and you believe the other side may object to it. There may be a certain statement that you want to have admitted and the other side is claiming it is hearsay, but you claim there may be an exception to the hearsay rule, and you want the court to give an advanced ruling on the admissibility.

It's particularly important to consider all possible motions in limine to be filed because you want to have advanced rulings on certain things, so you don't have to worry about it if it goes to trial. You want to raise it to the court, so the court is aware of it. Once certain evidence is given, you can't un-ring the bell. This is a way of having rulings made before someone spurts out certain inadmissible evidence that could be prejudicial or harmful.

A lot of care should be given to considering motions in limine and you should try to file as many as possible, provided that they are relevant. You want to find serious issues on the admissibility of evidence that need an advance ruling. It is particularly important to consider possible motions in limine to file before the trial or before the jury is empaneled.

Motions in limine are pretrial motions that are typically brought by one or both parties in order to narrow the issues to be presented to the jury.

When deciding a motion in limine, the court will consider the arguments and evidence presented by the parties, as well as the relevant legal standards. The court will also consider the potential impact of the evidence on the fairness of the trial, and whether the evidence is probative and relevant to the issues in the case.

The court may hold a hearing on the motion in limine to allow the parties to present arguments and evidence, or it may decide the motion based on written submissions from the parties.

If the court grants a motion in limine, it may issue an order that limits the admissibility of certain evidence or prohibits the parties from mentioning certain topics during trial. The court's ruling on a motion in limine is typically final, but the parties may seek reconsideration or appeal the ruling if they believe the court made an error.

It's important to note that the court's decision on a motion in limine is based on the evidence and arguments presented at the time of the motion, and the court may revisit the issue during trial if new evidence or circumstances arise.

Here are some typical motions in limine that may be filed in civil or criminal cases:

Motion in Limine to Exclude Irrelevant Evidence: This motion asks the court to exclude evidence that is not relevant to the case or that could confuse or mislead the jury.

Motion in Limine to Exclude Hearsay: This motion asks the court to exclude testimony or other evidence that is based on out-of-court statements, unless the statements fall within a recognized exception to the hearsay rule.

Motion in Limine to Exclude Expert Testimony: This motion asks the court to exclude expert testimony that is unreliable, irrelevant, or not based on sufficient facts or data.

Motion in Limine to Exclude Prejudicial Evidence: This motion asks the court to exclude evidence that is unduly prejudicial or that could inflame the passions of the jury, such as photographs or other graphic evidence.

Motion in Limine to Exclude Character Evidence:
This motion asks the court to exclude evidence of a party's character unless the evidence is directly relevant to the issues in the case.

Motion in Limine to Exclude Evidence Obtained Illegally: This motion asks the court to exclude evidence that was obtained in violation of the Fourth Amendment or other constitutional protections.

These are just a few examples of the types of motions in limine that may be filed in a particular case.

CHAPTER 18

GETTING ORGANIZED FOR TRIAL

There are several steps that lawyers can take to get organized for trial:

Review the case: The first step is to review the case thoroughly, including all documents, evidence, and witness statements. This will help the lawyer understand the strengths and weaknesses of the case.

Create a trial notebook: A trial notebook is a comprehensive folder or binder that contains all the information related to the case, including pleadings, discovery documents, witness statements, and evidence. The notebook should be organized in a logical manner and should be easy to navigate.

Prepare witness lists: The lawyer should prepare a list of witnesses they plan to call and provide the opposing counsel with a copy of the witness list. The witness list should include the name, contact information, and a brief summary of the testimony that the witness is expected to provide.

Prepare exhibit lists: The lawyer should prepare a list of exhibits they plan to introduce at trial and provide the opposing counsel with a copy of the exhibit list. The exhibit list should include a description of the exhibit and its relevance to the case.

Prepare trial briefs: Trial briefs summarize the legal arguments and facts of the case and provide a roadmap for the trial. The lawyer should prepare a trial brief for each issue that will be litigated at trial.

Prepare trial exhibits: The lawyer should organize and prepare all trial exhibits in advance. This includes making sure that all exhibits are marked, labeled, and ready to be introduced at trial.

Practice opening and closing statements: The lawyer should practice their opening and closing statements to ensure that they are effective and persuasive.

The best system I have seen for preparing for trial was created by an attorney named Robert Arns, Esq. and called *The Trial Wheel*. Mr. Arns suggests the trial lawyer create three trial binders with chapters. Volume includes: a to-do list; court calendar and a summary of the case.

Volume 2 includes: an economic analysis, a matrix of the motions in limine showing how the court ruled on each motion, a copy of the key jury instructions, the key demonstrative evidence, and a damage summary. Volume 3 includes: the verdict including special verdicts and information about the jurors and jury selection.

Mr. Arns suggests the lawyer create different witness binders for each witness. Each witness binder will include that witnesses' deposition including a deposition summary, a direct or cross examination outline, the key documents to present to that witness during their testimony, and any of their discovery response. The various binders should be color coded for easy identification. For example. the trial binders can be white three ring notebooks which the witness notebooks may be color coded with purple notebooks. The system also requires the attorney to maintain various other documents in manila folders including:

Exhibit lists

1. Jury instructions
2. Statement of the case
3. Witness lists
4. Legal research
5. Trial brief
6. Jury Questionnaire
7. Blow-ups of demonstrative evidence
8. Motions in limine
9. Discovery responses
10. Local rules

The goal of this system is to allow the trial lawyer to be able to find any piece of information in seconds and to create the impression of an organized and therefore reliable, competent, and trustworthy lawyer.

CHAPTER 19

DEVELOPING A VISUAL OVERVIEW

Developing a visual overview of a case can be a useful tool for organizing information and identifying key issues. Making a compelling PowerPoint presentation to show during your opening statement can be extremely important but before you can show the jury a visual or demonstrative aid, you need the consent of your opposing party's attorney.

You should provide your opposition a copy of what you intend to show during your opening before you get into the courtroom for your opening because if they object you will not normally have time to make any corrections to satisfy any of your opposition's objections.

Using a PowerPoint presentation during an opening statement can be an effective way to capture the attention of the jury and help them to better understand the key points of your case. The goal of your PowerPoint presentation is to help illustrate your key points, not to distract from them. Keep your slides simple and focused, with minimal text and clear visuals.

Visual aids such as photographs, diagrams, and charts can be a powerful way to communicate information and illustrate your points. Use visuals that are relevant to your case and that help to support your argument. Make sure that you are comfortable with the technology and that you have practiced your delivery in advance. Your PowerPoint should be a supplement to your opening statement, not a replacement for it.

Keep your PowerPoint focused on the key points of your opening statement and avoid getting sidetracked with extraneous information. Your PowerPoint should help to support your argument, not detract from your opening statement.

However, it's important to remember that a PowerPoint presentation is just one tool in your toolbox, and it's not always appropriate or necessary. The effectiveness of your opening statement will ultimately depend on your ability to connect with your audience, convey your message clearly, and make a strong first impression.

There are other tools for a visual presentation.

Flowcharts: A flowchart can be a helpful way to map out the sequence of events in a case. Start with the initial incident or dispute, and then use arrows and boxes to show the progression of the case through various stages (e.g., pleadings, discovery, trial, appeal).

Mind maps: A mind map is a type of diagram that can be used to organize information around a central theme or concept. Start by writing the key issue or question in the center of the page, and then use branches and sub-branches to map out related concepts and supporting arguments.

Timelines: A timeline can be a useful tool for visually representing the sequence of events in a case. Start with the initial incident or dispute, and then use a line or series of boxes to show the progression of key events (e.g., filings, hearings, decisions) over time.

Venn diagrams: A Venn diagram can be used to show the relationships between different concepts or arguments in a case. Start by identifying the key issues or arguments, and then use overlapping circles to show where they intersect and where they diverge.

Tables and matrices: A table or matrix can be a helpful tool for comparing and contrasting different arguments or positions in a case. Use rows and columns to identify the key issues or arguments, and then fill in the table with relevant information (e.g., legal authority, key facts).

By developing a visual overview of a case using one or more of these methods, you can create a clear and organized representation of the case that can help you to identify key issues, organize your arguments, and communicate your position more effectively.

CHAPTER 20

USING JURY AND TRIAL CONSULTANTS

■ WHEN TO CONSIDER USING A JURY AND TRIAL CONSULTANT

Jury and trial consultants assist lawyers and litigants in the jury selection process and provide guidance and advice during trial proceedings. Jury consultants may use a variety of techniques to gather information about potential jurors, including conducting surveys, analyzing public records, and conducting focus groups. They may also work with attorneys to develop strategies for presenting evidence and arguments to the jury.

Using a jury and trial consultant can significantly increase the cost of the litigation. While these consultants can give your client a definite advantage, they should only be used in high stakes and complex litigation. Jury and trial consultants use a variety of techniques to help attorneys and their clients prepare for trial. Some of the techniques they use include:

Jury selection: Jury consultants help attorneys select jurors who are likely to be sympathetic to their client's case. They analyze juror profiles, including demographic information, attitudes, and beliefs, to identify jurors who are most likely to be receptive to their arguments.

Focus groups: Focus groups are small groups of people who are brought together to discuss a particular topic. Jury consultants use focus groups to test trial strategies, assess the strengths and weaknesses of their client's case, and identify potential problems with their arguments.

In a focus group, a facilitator leads a discussion with a group of individuals who are typically representative of the target audience or potential jurors in a trial. The group is usually composed of 6-10 individuals, and they are selected based on specific criteria, such as demographics or their experiences related to the case. The facilitator guides the discussion and asks questions to encourage participants to share their thoughts, opinions, and attitudes towards the topic.

The aim of focus groups is to obtain insights into how people think and feel about a particular issue or topic, to better understand their motivations, and to uncover any potential biases or preconceptions. The information gathered from focus groups can be used by attorneys and their clients to develop more effective trial strategies, to identify potential issues with their arguments, and to improve their overall presentation.

Some benefits of focus groups include the ability to gather detailed and nuanced feedback, to identify common themes and trends, and to obtain feedback in a more natural and spontaneous setting than a survey or questionnaire.

> **Mock trials:** Mock trials are simulations of real trials that are conducted in a controlled environment prior to the actual trial. Mock trials involve presenting the evidence and arguments to a group of individuals who play the role of jurors and receiving feedback from them. These individuals may include legal professionalso, other attorneys, or members of the public who are similar to the likely jurors in the actual trial.

The main purpose of a mock trial is to test trial strategies, assess the strengths and weaknesses of a case, and identify potential problems with the arguments before the trial begins. Mock trials can help attorneys and their clients to understand how a jury may perceive their case, and to prepare for the challenges they may face in court.

During a mock trial, the attorneys present their case as they would in an actual trial, and the mock jurors deliberate and reach a verdict based on the evidence and arguments presented. Mock jurors may also be asked to provide feedback on various aspects of the trial, such as the strength of the evidence presented, the effectiveness of the attorneys' arguments, and the credibility of the witnesses.

Mock trials can provide attorneys and their clients with valuable insights into how to present their case most effectively in court. By identifying weaknesses in their arguments, attorneys can adjust their strategies and make improvements before the actual trial. This can increase the likelihood of a favorable outcome and reduce the risk of surprises or unexpected challenges during the trial.

Witness preparation: Jury consultants help witnesses prepare for their testimony by providing feedback on their delivery, helping them understand the key points they need to make, and coaching them on how to respond to difficult questions.

Trial graphics: Jury consultants create trial graphics, such as charts, diagrams, and animations, to help attorneys explain complex information to jurors in a clear and compelling way.

Shadow juries: Shadow juries are groups of individuals who observe a trial and provide feedback to the trial team throughout the trial proceedings. These individuals are typically selected to be representative of the actual jury, and they are often made up of friends, family members, or colleagues of the trial consultants or the legal team.

The purpose of a shadow jury is to provide the legal team with insights into how the actual jurors may be perceiving the case, the arguments being presented, and the evidence being presented. Shadow juries may be asked to complete surveys or questionnaires after each day of the trial, providing their feedback and impressions of the proceedings.

The feedback provided by the shadow jury can help the legal team to adjust their strategies and arguments in real-time, based on the feedback and reactions of the shadow jury. This can help to ensure that the legal team is presenting the strongest possible case to the actual jurors, and it can also help to identify potential issues with the case that may need to be addressed.

While shadow juries can be a valuable tool for the legal team, it is important to note that the feedback provided by the shadow jury may not always be completely representative of the actual jurors' opinions and reactions. Additionally, the use of a shadow jury can be expensive and time-consuming, and it may not be practical or feasible in all cases.

The main goal of a trial consultant is to help the legal team present the most effective case possible in court, by providing expert advice and assistance throughout the trial process. A trial consultant differs from a jury consultant in that a trial consultant focuses on preparing for trial by helping to organize evidence, develop trial strategies, and coach witnesses on how to testify effectively.

Trial consultants also assist attorneys in presenting their case in court by providing guidance on courtroom tactics, creating compelling trial graphics, and helping to prepare opening and closing arguments. They also assist in post-trial analysis in analyzing the outcome of the trial, identifying areas where the legal team could have improved their presentation, and developing strategies for future cases.

Overall, trial consultants play a critical role in helping attorneys and their clients present the most effective case possible in court. By providing expert advice and assistance throughout the trial process, trial consultants can help to increase the likelihood of a favorable outcome for their clients.

CHAPTER 21

FINAL STATUS CONFERENCE

A final status conference is a meeting held in a court case before the trial or hearing to discuss the final details of the case and prepare for trial. The conference is typically held after all the discovery and pre-trial motions have been completed, and the case is ready for trial.

During the final status conference, the judge, attorneys, and parties involved in the case discuss any outstanding issues, such as evidence, witnesses, and legal issues that need to be resolved before the trial. The parties may also discuss settlement options, which can help avoid the need for a trial.

The final status conference is important because it helps ensure that the trial proceeds smoothly and efficiently, and that both sides have an opportunity to resolve any outstanding issues before trial. It also allows the judge to assess the case and make any necessary rulings, such as on motions in limine or other procedural matters, which can help streamline the trial process.

All parties are required to file joint documents before the final status conference. This requires the parties to cooperate. The courts require civility between the parties and their attorneys. From my experience the best lawyers I have had as my opposing counsel have been courteous and professional. If they told you they would do something you could take them at their word. They were easy to work with, honest, cordial, and were willing to discuss and resolve issues fairly.

Unfortunately, the culture has become "win at all costs." Many lawyers you encounter cannot be trusted, which makes the trial experience unpleasant. My suggestion is to create a comfortable working relationship with your opposing counsel. It makes everybody's life easier and keeps the litigation costs down, which benefits the clients.

Joint Statement of the Case. One of the documents the attorneys are required to file for the final status conference is a joint statement of the case to be read to the jury.

The joint statement of the case is a document that is prepared by the parties involved in a legal case and submitted to the court prior to the final status conference. The purpose of the joint statement of the case is to provide the jurors and the court with a clear and concise summary of the case, including the key issues, evidence, and legal arguments.

The joint statement should be a short neutral statement and not show a bias or prejudice against or in favor of any party. The judge reads the joint statement of the case to the jury at the very beginning of the trial. If the joint statement shows a bias, it could appear the judge is giving greater weight to one party over another and could be a ground for appeal as a judicial error if the joint statement were prejudicial. A prejudicial joint statement can be grounds for appeal if it resulted in a miscarriage of justice.

Joint Exhibit list is a document that is typically prepared by the parties involved in a legal case and submitted to the court prior to the final status conference. The purpose of the joint exhibit list is to provide the court and the opposing party with a list of all the exhibits that will be presented at trial.

At the final status conference, the joint exhibit list is typically discussed by the parties and the court. The joint exhibit list can help to ensure that both parties are aware of the evidence that will be presented at trial and can help to avoid surprises during the trial.

The joint exhibit list typically includes a list of all the exhibits that will be presented at trial, including documents, photographs, videos, and other physical evidence. The list may also include a brief description of each exhibit, as well as any objections that either party may have to the admissibility of the exhibit.

Federal courts usually require each side to state their objection to any exhibits on the joint exhibit list. If a party fails to state an objection the court will automatically admit the exhibit. This could be devastating for your case at trial. Take great pains to review your opposing counsel's list of exhibits and make sure you timely file objections. Objections can range from lack of authentication, lack of foundation and any permissible evidentiary objection including hearsay, legal relevance under Fed. Rule Evid. 403, improper opinion or improper character evidence.

Federal Rule of Evidence Rule 403 is a rule that governs the admission of evidence in a trial or hearing in federal court. Rule 403 allows the court to exclude relevant evidence if its probative value is substantially outweighed by the danger of unfair prejudice, confusion of the issues, misleading the jury, undue delay, wasting time, or needlessly presenting cumulative evidence.

In other words, even if evidence is relevant to the case, it may still be excluded if it could unfairly prejudice one of the parties, confuse the issues, or waste time. The rule provides the judge with discretion to determine whether the potential harm caused by admitting the evidence outweighs its probative value.

When applying Rule 403, the court must weigh the probative value of the evidence against the potential harm it may cause. The court may consider factors such as the nature of the evidence, the strength of the evidence, the importance of the evidence to the case, the potential for the evidence to mislead the jury or confuse the issues, and the potential for the evidence to cause unfair prejudice.

Rule 403 applies to all types of evidence, including witness testimony, physical evidence, and documentary evidence. It is designed to ensure that trials are fair and efficient by excluding evidence that is more prejudicial than probative.

The joint exhibit list is an important document because it helps to ensure that the trial proceeds smoothly and efficiently. By providing a list of all the exhibits that will be presented at trial, the joint exhibit list helps to avoid delays and confusion during the trial and can help to ensure that the evidence is presented in a clear and organized manner.

Joint Witness list is a document that is typically prepared by the parties involved in a legal case and submitted to the court prior to the final status conference. The purpose of the joint witness list is to provide the court and the opposing party with a list of all the witnesses that will be called to testify at trial.

At the final status conference, the joint witness list is typically discussed by the parties and the court. The joint witness list can help to ensure that both parties are aware of the witnesses that will be called to testify at trial and can help to avoid surprises during the trial.

The joint witness list typically includes a list of all the witnesses that will be called to testify at trial, including the name, address, and contact information for each witness. The list may also include a brief summary of the witness's testimony, as well as any objections that either party may have to the testimony of a particular witness.

An important aspect of the joint witness list is to list the amount of time each party will need in their direct examination, cross examination and any re-direct or re-cross. This will assist the court and the parties for predicting the anticipated length of the trial.

The joint witness list is an important document because it helps to ensure that the trial proceeds smoothly and efficiently. By providing a list of all the witnesses that will be called to testify at trial, the joint witness list helps to avoid delays and confusion during the trial and can help to ensure that the testimony is presented in a clear and organized manner. Additionally, the joint witness list can help the parties to identify potential areas of agreement or disagreement, which can be helpful in preparing for trial and potentially negotiating a settlement.

Trial Brief is a written document submitted to the court before a trial that outlines the legal arguments, evidence, and other important information related to the case. It helps the judge to understand the issues at hand and the positions of each party, which can streamline the trial process and lead to a more efficient and effective trial. A trial brief may also contain other important information, such as a list of witnesses and exhibits, a proposed schedule for the trial, and any other relevant information that the judge may need to know.

Special Verdict form is a document used in a trial that requires the jury to answer specific questions about the case based on the evidence presented. A special verdict form helps to clarify the issues that the jury needs to decide by providing specific questions for them to answer. This can be especially helpful in complex cases where there are multiple legal issues or factual disputes.

By providing specific questions for the jury to answer, a special verdict form can help to focus the jury's attention on the key issues in the case. This can help to ensure that the jury reaches a well-informed and thoughtful decision.

A special verdict form can also be useful in facilitating appellate review of the trial court's decision. By providing a clear record of the jury's findings, a special verdict form can help to ensure that any appellate review is based on a complete and accurate record of the trial proceedings.

Here is an example of a Special Verdict form I submitted in a recent case. The names have been changed.

We answer the questions submitted to us as follows on Plaintiff Sam Peterson and Podunk Widget LLC's complaint for trademark infringement and unfair competition:

1. Is Sam Peterson and Podunk Widget LLC's trademark "Electric Switch" generic?

    ____Yes ____No

If you answered Question 1 "Yes" then go to the end and sign and return this form. If you answered "No" then answer Question 2.

2. Is Sam Peterson and Podunk Widget LLC's trademark "Electric Switch" descriptive without proof of secondary meaning?

    ____Yes ____No

If you answered Question 2 "Yes" then go to the end and sign and return this form. If you answered "No" then answer Question 3.

3. Is Sam Peterson the owner of the trademark "Electric Switch?"

    ____Yes ____No

If you answered Question 3 "No "then go to the end and sign and return this form. If you answered "Yes" then answer Question 4.

4. Did the defendants use Electric Switch, or a mark similar to Electric Switch without the consent of the plaintiff in a manner that is likely to cause confusion among ordinary consumers as to the source, sponsorship, affiliation, or approval of the goods?
_____Yes _____No

If you answered Question 4 "No "then go to the end and sign and return this form. If you answered "Yes" then answer Question 5.

5. Did Sam Peterson and Podunk Widget LLC's prove that the defendants engaged in trademark infringement?
_____Yes _____No

If you answered Question 5 "No "then go to the end and sign and return this form. If you answered "Yes" then answer Question 6.

6. Did Sam Peterson and Podunk Widget LLC's prove that the defendants engaged in unfair competition?
_____Yes _____No

If you answered Question 6 "No "then go to the end and sign and return this form. If you answered "Yes" then answer Question 7.

7. Does the defense of unclean hands preclude plaintiffs from prevailing in this case?
_____Yes _____No

If you answered Question 7 "Yes" then go to the end and sign and return this form. If you answered "No" then answer Question 8.

8. Does the defense of the first sale doctrine preclude plaintiffs from prevailing in this case?

_____Yes _____No

If you answered Question 8 "Yes" then go to the end and sign and return this form. If you answered "No" then answer Question 9.

9. Did plaintiff Sam Peterson suffer any damages from the defendants' infringement?

_____Yes _____No

If you answered Question 9 "No" then go to the end and sign and return this form. If you answered "Yes" then answer Question 10.

10. State the amount of damages plaintiff suffered.

Lost profits _____

Damage to reputation _____

The injury to or loss to plaintiff's goodwill _____

Other (specify) _____

Signed: _____ Presiding Juror

The Special Verdict in the above example is designed to force the plaintiff to overcome every obstacle toward a jury award. If the jury answers "yes" to Question number 1, the plaintiff loses on this claim. If the jury answer "yes" to the second question again there is a defense verdict. There is a defense verdict if the jury answers "no" to Questions 3, 4, 5, or 6.

Plaintiffs usually prefer a general verdict, while the defense usually prefers a special verdict. A general verdict is a type of verdict that is rendered by a jury in a trial. In a civil case, a general verdict is typically either in favor of the plaintiff or in favor of the defendant and states an amount if the verdict favors the plaintiff. In a general verdict the jury does not answer any questions.

A general verdict differs from a special verdict, which is a verdict that requires the jury to make specific findings of fact and answer specific questions posed by the court. Special verdicts are favored in cases where the facts are complex, or the legal issues are particularly nuanced.

A general verdict may be challenged on appeal if there are errors in the trial or if the verdict is not supported by the evidence presented at trial. However, the scope of the review on appeal is limited, and the appellate court will generally defer to the jury's findings of fact and interpretation of the law, unless there was a clear error or abuse of discretion by the trial court.

CHAPTER 22

WRITING A WINNING BRIEF

■ THE INTRODUCTION

A professionally written brief is essential if your case is to be successful. I find that most of the briefs I read suffer from the same shortcoming; they are boring. You need to capture the attention of the judge or law clerk who will be reading the brief by starting with a crisp, short, and compelling introduction.

The introduction should briefly describe the parties involved in the litigation and briefly describe the dispute. Once you have listed the essential elements in a conversational manner, add a pithy short summary of the essence of the controversy that will grab the attention of the reader. The following is an example of an appellate brief highlighting that style for an introduction.

"This appeal arises following the granting of summary judgment on contentious litigation over a performance and payment bond claim

on a public works construction project. On one side is Plaintiff/
Appellant ABC Electric Inc. and its founder and owner Serge Bolt
(Serge is a good name for an electrician). On the other side is the
Appellee M&B Surety, the surety that issued the payment and per-
formance bond.

This matter arose out of the Angeles Unified School District
seeking bids from contractors for the construction of a middle school
called the Hulk Middle school. The plot line of this controversy is
disturbing: Four years after an experienced and competent contractor
who successfully completed a public works construction project is
forced to defend his stellar work from baseless accusations brought
by less than competent individuals with hidden agendas."

After your short introduction follow up with what you are asking
from the court.

"This summary judgment must be overturned for four independent reasons:

First, ABC and Surety executed an Agreement of Indemnity
as a condition to obtain the performance bond. Paragraph 4 of the
Agreement of Indemnity states that the "Surety is hereby authorized,
in its sole discretion, or make or guarantee advances or *loans* for the
purposes of the contract...and the Indemnitors agree...that such loans
unless repaid with legal interest shall be conclusively presumed to
be an Indemnity obligation..." Because M&B Surety could decide
whether or not to loan ABC the $150,000 in its *sole discretion*, M&B
Surety had a duty to exercise its discretion in good faith. [see *Carma
Developers (Cal.), Inc. v. Marathon Dev. Cal., Inc.,*("*Carma*") 2 Cal.
4th 342, 350, 6

Cal. Rptr. 2d 467, 469, 826 P.2d 710, 712 (1992) holding that
"the covenant of good faith finds particular application in situations
where one party is invested with a discretionary power affecting the
rights of another. This power must be exercised in good faith."]

Carma established that M&B Surety owed ABC and Serge a duty to act in good faith when it denied Serge's request to lend ABC the $150,000 to settle this case. A surety also has a duty to mitigate damages for its bond principal. This duty arises from the surety's obligation to act in good faith and deal fairly with both the principal and the obligee (the party protected by the bond). [see *Mass. Bonding & Ins. Co. v. Osborne*, 233 Cal. App. 2d 648, 650 (1965)]

Second, a material issue of fact exists on whether M&B Surety acted in good faith when it denied ABC's request to contribute $150,000 toward the settlement. M&B Surety was joint and severally liable with ABC on Angeles's $3 million bond claim; it had the Collateral Security Agreement secured by Serge's personal residence; and it breached its duty to mitigate damages thereby exposing Serge to an unreasonable peril. When M&B Surety's attorney Frank Johnson was asked why he attended the mediation if M&B Surety had no intention of contributing any money toward the settlement his arrogant response was "I came for the lunch" and "why should we, I've got your house."

Third, even assuming M&B Surety was not bound by the holding in *Carma*, M&B Surety still had an implied obligation to advance reasonable sums toward the settlement because it had a prior agreement with Serge where it advanced money to settle a bond claim on a San Diego project and it entered into the Collateral Security Agreement where it obtained a deed of trust on Serge's personal residence. Serge *reasonably expected* that M&B Surety would advance the $150,000 to settle the Angeles claim. The conduct of the parties created an implied covenant which obligated M&B Surety to contribute money toward this settlement.

Fourth, M&B Surety argues that ABC needs to show that Angeles "would have" accepted the $400,000 if it was timely tendered. In order to show Angeles "would have" accepted the $400,000 there was a condition that the $400,000 be actually tendered. M&B Surety was responsible for making sure that condition failed."

The introduction of your brief uses the same psychology you use in your opening statement. and should be written in a manner to keep the attention of the reader. I have a colleague who was an excellent lawyer. He wanted to be a judge but did not have any political connections and went to work as a clerk for the California Court of Appeal. As the clerk he wrote between 400-500 opinions which became the opinions of the Court.

His job was to read the opening briefs, opposition briefs and reply to briefs. He would conduct his own research and write a draft opinion. He would meet with the judge assigned to the case and present his opinion. Out of the 400-500 opinions he wrote only two required a different result.

Nobody knows better how to present a compelling appellate brief than this individual with all his experience. We worked together preparing a brief I filed in the ninth circuit court of appeal. He confirmed the importance of a succinct and compelling introduction. The introduction was followed by a list of the *Players*. I learned the law clerks reading the brief liked having a list of all the parties mentioned in the brief as a reference on their roles in the case. The list of players was followed by a listing of the issues, statement of the facts, procedural history, standard of review, summary of argument, argument, and conclusion.

■ USE A NOVELISTIC STYLE IN YOUR BRIEF

Write in a conversational tone. All too often the fact section in briefs contain non-stop conclusions and accusations about your opposing party and contain a one-sided narrative of the events. Sometimes it is all too obvious the facts are skewed. The judge or clerk reading your brief that shows an unfair recitation of the facts will become skeptical. A more persuasive approach is if the facts in your brief read more like a newspaper article where the facts are just that; 'fact" not a hyperbolic version of events.

Strive for a novelistic approach in your writing. A novelistic approach to brief writing involves using storytelling techniques typically found in novels to create a compelling and persuasive brief. This approach can help the writer to engage the reader and make complex legal arguments more accessible.

Just like in a novel, a brief should have a clear beginning, middle, and end. This structure can help to guide the reader through the arguments and keep them engaged. Novelistic writing often relies on rich, descriptive language to create a vivid sense of place and character. In a legal brief, this could mean using powerful metaphors or analogies to help illustrate complex legal concepts.

While legal briefs are not typically centered around characters, a novelistic approach may involve creating persuasive and relatable characters to help illustrate the impact of the case. Dialogue can be a powerful tool for conveying information and building tension. In a brief, dialogue could be used to illustrate a point, provide a counter-argument, or highlight the stakes of the case.

Novelistic writing often seeks to evoke an emotional response in the reader. A brief written with a novelistic approach might aim to connect with the reader on a personal level by highlighting the real-world consequences of the case.

■ AVOID LENGTHY CASE ANALYSIS AND CITATIONS

It is generally a good idea to avoid lengthy case analysis in your brief, as it can distract from the central arguments and make the document overly long and difficult to read.

Here are a few tips for minimizing case analysis in your brief:

- Rather than trying to analyze every case that might be relevant to your argument, focus on the few key cases that are most important. Choose cases that are directly on point, or that are particularly influential in the relevant legal area. Instead of providing a full analysis of each case, consider using brief summaries to highlight the key holdings or facts. This can help to quickly establish the relevance of the case without getting bogged down in details.

- When discussing cases in your brief, focus on the most important points that support your argument. Be selective in your analysis and avoid discussing extraneous details that are not central to your position. While case law is an important part of legal argumentation, it is possible to over-rely on it in a brief. Consider using other sources of authority, such as statutes or regulations, to support your arguments when appropriate.

- The mistake that many lawyers make is they claim a certain case is directly on point and therefore dispositive of their motion. They then summarize a long sequence of facts by taking direct quotes from this key case. Instead of forcing the reader of your brief to read through pages discussing every detail of a case that may only be superficially related, the better approach is to use your own words and your thoughts when you discuss the case authority. This makes your brief more personal and authentic.

- Above all, strive to be concise and to the point in your brief. Use clear and straightforward language to communicate your arguments and avoid unnecessary repetition or redundancy. By minimizing case analysis in your brief and focusing on the most important points, you can create a more persuasive and reader-friendly document that effectively communicates your legal position.

■ ALWAYS FILE A REPLY BRIEF

If you don't file a reply brief, the judge reading the brief will wonder why. This is the perfect opportunity to get to the final word. In your relief brief make sure you acknowledge each of your opponent's arguments in their opposition and carefully explain why she is still missing the point. Systematically attack the opposition papers point by point in a numbered reply brief.

Read the cases cited in the opposition and look for a common thread in their argument. Attack each case or point out the common thread of your opposition cited and address them collectively by pointing out any error and why their authority and argument is flawed. It is extremely important to address every case authority cited by your opposition and distinguish that case from the authority you cited.

Your reply brief is your opportunity to focus the court once again on your strong point and winning argument. Don't pass up that opportunity.

CHAPTER 23

THE TRIAL

■ **A TRIAL IS LIKE TAKING A COURSE IN COLLEGE**

Michael Stein, who teaches continuing education, has a remarkably interesting approach that he tells jurors during his opening statement. He tells them that a trial is like taking a course in college. The jury selection process is the equivalent to the college admission process. That is when you determine who is going to take the class. The next phase is the opening statement which is a brief summary of evidence that will be presented during the trial.

That is like the course outline or the syllabus where the students get an outline of the topics. The prospective jurors are given a summary of what they can expect as jurors, what they are going to hear and what the case is about. After that, you are getting into the witnesses, who are the guest speakers and may include expert witnesses who have special knowledge on a particular subject. These speakers will talk about documents, exhibits, summaries, and the facts and events to which they witnessed and may include giving opinions.

The next phase is the final exam review course, which is the closing argument. The jurors are going to take a final exam. The final exam is the jury verdict form. The jury takes the verdict form into the jury room when they start deliberations. They are required to answer questions to produce a verdict. This is an interesting way of presenting a case, because it presents the lawyer more as an instructor than an aggressive representative.

■ OPENING STATEMENT

Some people think the opening statement is one of the most important aspects of a trial and jury consultants and social psychologists have done studies that show that most people make up their mind early, during the opening statement. Other jury consultants tell me that they believe juries make up their minds after the cross examination of the key witness, which is after the opening statement. There are different theories, but recently I saw an interview with a highly intelligent woman, who is a film professor at Yale. She was saying that the opening scenes are one of the most important parts of movies because they set the stage for the balance of the film.

She gave three examples of opening scenes in movies that she thought were immensely powerful. One was the movie, directed by Steven Spielberg, called Schindler's List. The opening scene starts out focusing on a candle and smoke coming up from the candle, and the camera pans out to reveal a Jewish family on a Sabbath, saying a prayer and lighting a candle. Then, the candle goes out and you see smoke going up as it segues into a train moving into a concentration camp, with the smoke of the train going up. You then see a businessman, but you don't see his face, you only see his hand as he is walking, and he is enormously powerful. It turns out to be Schindler, who is played by Liam Neeson. The film is powerful because the opening scene immediately grabs you.

An opening scene in a movie is certainly similar to an opening statement at trial. You want to really grab the parties with your emotional reaction of what the case is about to get them interested. I used to start my opening statements by thanking the jurors, identifying myself and who I represent, and then I'd spend about five minutes talking about things that really weren't that interesting. I've realized that a better approach is to use emotion in the opening statement to grab the attention of the jurors at the earliest time possible. There are other theories about using primacy and recency in arguments and statements, and it means that people remember the first thing they hear and they remember the last thing they hear.

You have to make an exceptionally good first impression in your opening statement. Go immediately to the emotional aspect, talking about the triggering event and the emotional appeal it had or the emotional effect it had on your client. Then, bring up the tagline at the very earliest possible time.

The opening statement needs to have an emotional response and you are also going to tell the jury the factual background and the evidence. You don't want to overstate your case, but you want to make an emotional impact on the jury and tell them the story of what happened. Legal scholars suggest the best opening statements tell a captivating story to the jurors. People are wired to respond to stories, and a well-crafted story can be very persuasive. Use storytelling techniques to create a narrative that engages the jury's emotions and draws them into the case.

Here is an example of the start of a compelling opening statement: "In early July, in exceptional heat, towards the evening, a young man left the garret he was renting on S_Y Lane, stepped outside, and slowly, as if two minds, set off towards K_n Bridge. He'd successfully avoided meeting his landlady on the stairs. His garret was right beneath the eaves of a tall, five-story building and resembled a cupboard more than it did a room."

If this looks familiar you only need to read the opening lines from Fyodor Dostoevsky's *Crime and Punishment*. The best way to learn how to give a compelling story in your opening statement is by reading classic literature.

A compelling opening statement is important because it sets the tone for the rest of your presentation, speech, or argument. In order to grab the jurors' attention use a powerful opening line or anecdote to grab the attention of your audience. This could be a surprising statistic, a thought-provoking question, a humorous story, or a bold statement that challenges conventional thinking.

State your main argument or point in your opening statement by clearly relaying the main argument or point you will be making. This helps your audience understand the purpose of your presentation and what they can expect to learn.

Give your audience some context or background information that helps them understand the topic you will be discussing. This could be a brief history of the issue, an overview of the current state of affairs, or a summary of previous research or findings.

Nearly every trial these days uses technology to bring your points home. I strongly suggest using visual aids such as slides, images, or videos to help illustrate your points and capture the attention of your audience. Programs like *Trial Director* or *PowerPoint* are particularly effective.

Remember the lesson on using pathos and incorporate those theories into your opening statement. A good opening statement must appeal to the emotions of the jury. If you want to craft an opening statement that appeals to the emotions of the jury, here are some tips:

Use vivid and descriptive language: Use language that paints a picture in the minds of the jury, making the situation more real and relatable. For example, instead of saying "the victim was killed," you could say "the victim's life was brutally taken away, leaving her family devastated and broken."

Highlight the human aspect of the case: Bring the focus back to the people involved in the case, whether it's the victim, the defendant, or their families. Emphasize the impact the case has had on their lives and how it has affected them emotionally.

Use rhetorical devices: Rhetorical devices like repetition, alliteration, and rhetorical questions can be used to add emphasis and drama to your opening statement. For example, you could say "The defendant took everything from the victim. Her life. Her dreams. Her future."

Build tension and anticipation: Use your opening statement to build anticipation for what's to come in the trial. You can do this by introducing key pieces of evidence, witnesses, or arguments that will be presented during the trial.

Appeal to the values and beliefs of the jurors: Consider what values and beliefs the jurors may hold and try to appeal to them in your opening statement. For example, if the case involves a child victim, you could appeal to the jurors' sense of protection and responsibility towards children.

While it's important to appeal to the emotions of the jury, you must also stay within the bounds of the law and present a fair and objective case. Use your opening statement to engage the jurors and create a connection with them, but always keep the focus on the evidence and facts of the case.

When delivering an opening statement, there are several things you want to avoid in order to keep the jurors engaged and focused on the case. Here are some things you *don't* want to do in an opening statement:

Make unsupported assertions: Avoid making unsupported assertions, as they can weaken your credibility and come across as manipulative. Instead, stick to the facts and evidence that will be presented during the trial.

Use inflammatory language: Using language that is overly emotional or inflammatory can backfire and turn the jurors off. Stick to a calm and professional tone and focus on the facts of the case.

Attack the other side: Avoid attacking the other side in your opening statement, as this can create a defensive reaction and make it harder to establish a productive dialogue during the trial.

Make promises you can't keep: Don't make promises you can't keep, such as promising to present evidence that is not admissible in court. This can harm your credibility and weaken your case.

Overwhelm the jurors: Keep your opening statement concise and focused on the key points of the case. Avoid overwhelming the jurors with too much information or technical jargon that they may not understand.

The opening statement is your chance to set the tone for the trial and establish a connection with the jurors. By avoiding these common pitfalls, you can present a clear, compelling, and objective case that is more likely to persuade the jurors.

If you represent the defendant and are giving your opening statement after your opposing counsel gave their opening statement you may want to point out inconsistencies in the opponent's opening statement. By doing so, a lawyer can establish their own credibility and show that they have carefully reviewed the evidence.

You can set the tone for the trial by highlighting weaknesses in the opponent's case early on, which can influence the jury's perception of the case. The opening statement is also an opportunity for lawyers to preview the evidence they will present during the trial. By identifying inconsistencies in the opponent's opening statement, a lawyer can begin to prepare their cross- examination strategy. Pointing out inconsistencies in the opponent's case can put pressure on them to provide a more coherent and consistent narrative through-out the trial.

Not all inconsistencies in an opponent's opening statement will be relevant or persuasive to the jury. You must be careful not to over-state the significance of minor inconsistencies or make arguments that are unsupported by the evidence. The effectiveness of pointing out inconsistencies will ultimately depend on the specific circum-stances of the case and the strength of the evidence presented.

Remember that a compelling opening statement should grab your audience's attention, clearly state your main argument or point, provide context, use visual aids if appropriate, and be well-rehearsed.

CHAPTER 24

DIRECT EXAMINATION

Direct examination is when you put your witness on the stand to support your case. You put forth evidence, facts, and documents that are consistent with your theory of the case. It's a good idea to start with your strongest witness. People tend to remember the first things they hear, so start strong. Direct examinations are not always easy because you can't ask leading questions. The witness doesn't always understand what you are trying to ask them.

■ ONLY NON-LEADING QUESTIONS

A question on direct examination (e.g. a non-leading question) requires the question to start with: who, what, when why or how. Sounds easy but you will be surprised at the difficulty many lawyers have framing a question that is not leading. Examples of non-leading questions, which will not draw objections during direct examination include:

- "How did you learn that Jimmy was in the hospital?"
- "What was the first thing you did after you witnessed the accident?"
- "Why did you call the police?"
- "Who was with you when you discovered the theft?"
- "When did you realize the defendant infringed on your trademark?
- "How did you learn that?"
- "What is your name?" which is an open-ended question while "Your name is John Smith, isn't it? is a leading question. It suggests the answer.

A leading question is a type of question that suggests a particular answer or implies a desired response. In other words, it "leads" the person being questioned to a particular answer, rather than allowing them to give an independent and unbiased response. Leading questions do not merely suggest the answer: they declare the answer.

Leading questions are typically designed to influence the person being questioned in a particular way, often to support a particular argument or line of reasoning. A lawyer on direct examination is generally precluded from using leading questions while an attorney during cross examination should only use leading questions.

Examples of leading questions include:

- "Isn't it true that you saw the defendant commit the crime?"
- "Don't you agree that the plaintiff was at fault in the accident?"
- "Wouldn't you say that the defendant's actions were negligent?"

In each of these examples, the question implies a particular answer and may be objected to by opposing counsel as a leading question if given on direct examination. A leading question allows the attorney performing the cross examination to be effectively testifying. Most of the answers in response to the lawyer's leading question will be either "Yes" or "No" and gives no room to explain or take control away from the attorney who is engaged in cross examination.

Effective direct examination requires thorough preparation on the part of the attorney. They must be familiar with the witness's background, the facts of the case, and the specific testimony they are seeking to elicit. Failure to adequately prepare can result in a disjointed and ineffective direct examination.

Direct examination is a skill that takes practice to develop. Inexperienced attorneys may struggle to ask effective questions, manage objections from opposing counsel, and keep the testimony focused on the relevant issues.

Direct examination is limited to the scope of the witness's personal knowledge and experience. Attorneys must carefully craft their questions to ensure that the witness is providing relevant and admissible testimony, without straying into areas that are beyond the witness's personal knowledge or expertise.

■ THE HOSTILE WITNESS

You usually want to call friendly witnesses for your direct examination. If a witness is "hostile" you can ask the judge to allow you to cross examine the witness even though you were the one calling the witness.

Witnesses may be uncooperative or evasive, making it difficult for the attorney to elicit clear and concise answers to their questions. In some cases, witnesses may even be hostile to the party calling them and intentionally give unhelpful or misleading testimony. A hostile witness is a witness who exhibits a negative or uncooperative attitude towards the party calling them to testify, or who gives testimony that is unfavorable or inconsistent with their prior statements or the evidence presented in the case.

When a witness is deemed hostile, the party calling them to testify may be permitted to cross-examine the witness in a more aggressive or confrontational manner and may even be allowed to ask leading questions (which are typically not allowed during direct examination).

To establish that a witness is hostile, the party calling them to testify may need to demonstrate that the witness is biased against them, has a personal interest in the outcome of the case, or has previously given inconsistent or contradictory statements about the matter at hand.

For example, if a witness has given a prior statement to the police or in a deposition that conflicts with their testimony at trial, the opposing party may argue that the witness is being hostile and request to cross- examine them in a more aggressive manner. This can help to challenge the witness's credibility and potentially undermine their testimony.

■ KEEP YOUR CLIENT'S DIRECT EXAMINATION INTERESTING

When you call your client on direct examination the challenge is to keep his or her testimony interesting. When you ask an open-ended question, the person responding often gives lengthy run-on narrative answers that can bore the jurors. Keep in mind the jurors are being forced to sit in the trial and may not be enthralled with your case. Consequently, they may have short attention spans.

If every one of your questions is calling for a lengthy answer, after a few seconds, most jurors won't pay attention to it. The way to keep a juror's attention on direct examination is to try to create a rhythm or cadence by starting with questions that require a short answer, followed by a long answer. For example, a musical opera that will keep your attention is a series of short notes followed by a long note; consider Beethoven's Ninth Symphony *Ode to Joy* that goes-ba ba ba baaaaa. Ask a series of yes or no questions, then ask for an explanation or elaboration.

The way you keep their attention is by putting *forward motion* into your direct examination by the technique of asking a series of leading questions that take only one or two words to answer followed by a question that takes much longer to answer. Sometimes a court will allow an attorney to ask questions on direct examination to ask limited leading questions.

Generally, leading questions are not allowed during direct examination, as the purpose of direct examination is to elicit testimony from the witness in a neutral and non-leading manner. However, there are certain limited circumstances where leading questions may be permitted during direct examination.

Leading questions may be used during direct examination to establish preliminary matters, such as a witness's name, address, or occupation or to questions where there is no dispute to the facts. Leading questions may also be allowed if a witness has trouble recalling certain details or events, the attorney may be permitted to ask leading questions in order to refresh the witness's memory.

In all cases, the judge has discretion to allow or disallow leading questions during direct examination, and opposing counsel may object to any leading questions that are deemed improper or inappropriate.

An example of how you can create *forward motion* on direct examination by the pace of your questioning is as follows:

1. "Do you remember the morning of October 3rd? "Yes"
2. "You got up at about 10:00? "Yes"
3. "Walked down to 6th and Olive?" "I did"
4. "Something happened when you were standing there?" "Indeed"
5. "Tell the jury what happened?"

At this point, the witness goes into great detail how she observed a red Buick go through the red light at such a fast speed she thought someone was going to get killed.

If this were a music score it would sound or look like: ba, ba, ba, baaaaaaaaaaaaaaaaaaaa. The cadence of this question will keep the jurors' attention during otherwise boring direct examination.

CHAPTER 25

CROSS EXAMINATION

One important aspect of a common law trial is the ability to cross examine witnesses. Cross examination is the guarantee of reliability and fairness. Cross examination is designed to persuade the judge or the jury that the opposing witness is not worth believing. During cross-examination, the opposing side's attorney has the opportunity to ask the witness questions aimed at testing the witness's credibility and the accuracy of their testimony. This can be particularly important if the witness's testimony is the only evidence available to support a particular side of the case.

The cross-examination can also help to uncover any inconsistencies or contradictions in the witness's testimony, which can be used to undermine the witness's credibility and weaken their testimony. This can be particularly effective if the inconsistencies are significant or if they call into question the witness's ability to accurately recall events.

In summary, the cross-examination of a key witness can be a critical part of a trial, as it provides an opportunity to challenge the credibility and accuracy of the witness's testimony and potentially undermine their contribution to the case.

■ THE THREE RULES OF CROSS EXAMINATION

Many jury consultants will tell you that juries decide cases after the cross examination of a key witness. Cross examination is particularly important. The concept of cross examination is using deductive reasoning to go from very general to extremely specific conclusions. There is an excellent book by Larry Posner and Roger Dodd called Cross Examination: Science and Techniques. It outlines three rules of cross examination.

> **Rule One** is that you only ask leading questions. That is how it differs from direct examination.

> **Rule Two** is that your questions have one fact per question. You want short, yes or no questions, so you can easily take the jury from a very general to a specific conclusion.

> **Rule Three** is that you break cross examination into a series of logical progressions to each specific goal.

■ KNOW WHERE TO STAND DURING YOUR DIRECT AND CROSS EXAMINATION

During your direct examination you want the jury to focus on the witness. He tells the story and gives the facts. During your direct examination of your witness try to stand as close to the jury as the court will allow. By standing close to the jury during your direct examination, the jury will be looking at the witness who will be facing them when testifying. They can look into his eyes and body language more easily than if he was looking away from the jury.

On cross examination, by asking leading questions, you are able to control the witness. During cross examination try to stand as far away from the jury the court will allow. This way the juries' focus will be on you as the attorney who will be controlling the examination and not on the witness. You want the jury to be hearing your questions as the evidence. It is like you are testifying and not the witness.

■ USE DEDUCTIVE REASONING ON CROSS EXAMINATION

In a cross-examination, deductive reasoning can be a powerful tool to help lawyers establish their case or undermine the credibility of the opposing side. Start with very general questions, leading to a specific conclusion. Each question should have one fact. You begin by identifying a general premise that is relevant to your case. For example, if you are arguing that a defendant is guilty of a crime, you might start with the premise that "people who commit crimes leave evidence behind."

Next, apply the premise to the specific facts of the case. For example, you might ask the witness, "Did you find any evidence at the scene of the crime that might link the defendant to the crime?"

If the witness's answer contradicts the premise, this could be an opportunity to challenge their credibility or to weaken their testimony. For example, if the witness claims that they found no evidence at the scene of the crime, but the defendant's DNA was found there, you might ask the witness to explain this discrepancy.

Follow up with additional questions that help to clarify the witness's testimony and expose any inconsistencies. For example, you might ask the witness, "Can you explain why you didn't find any evidence, despite the fact that the defendant's DNA was present?"

Repeat the process with other premises and facts relevant to your case. By using deductive reasoning in cross-examination, you can build a persuasive argument and challenge the opposing side's case.

■ CROSS EXAMINATION OUTLINE

I create a sheet for cross examinations with three columns. I have my questions in the center column, and I list the reference where I find the information in the left column that I can refer to if the witness gives contradictory testimony. This contradictory evidence can be his deposition with the page and line where he gave a previous answer. If he says something different, then I can read from his deposition to contradict his testimony at trial. Below is an example of a cross examination sheet used at trial.

What follows is a copy of the one page-one fact approach to cross examination. The heading is ultimate fact you want to accomplish on cross examination of this witness. You start with a single leading question containing a single fact. The column on the left is where you list where you can find this fact if the witness does not answer properly. This is used for impeachment.

You want the witness to answer every question with either a "yes "or a "no" because that way you control the witness. By controlling the witness as if you as the lawyer are testifying.

The leading questions continue one fact at a time until you reach the conclusion where Newton admits that he waited about two years to raise the claim you were owed money on the Boxwood project.

	NEWTON GOT PAID IN FULL ON REDWOOD	
	You claim you were a partner in the Redwood or Boxwood project	
Newton depo. page 24 line 7-11	You are claiming you are entitled to profits from the Redwood project	
Ex. 24- commission summary	Point III received $159,637 as its share of the commissions on the Boxwood project	
	You got that for guaranteeing the loan on the Boxwood project	
Kristine declaration par. 12	You received your share of the commissions in April, 2012	
	You received your share of the commissions more than 4 years ago	
	You knew the total amount of money that went into Point III from the Boxwood project	
	You received 20% of those funds	
	Norm and Phil received the balance	

Ex. 31-Newton letter dated Fed. 2016	You never complained that you were owed more money on the Boxwood project until February 2016. MORE THAN 4 YEARS LATER	
	You never complained that you were owed more money on the Boxwood project until after Bridgepoint and Norm sued you in 2014.	
	You waited about 2 years after Norm and Bridgepoint sued you to raise the claim you were owed money on the Boxwood project	

■ LOOPING

The technique called "looping" is a technique used on cross examination to draw the jury's attention to a particular fact. Some facts are more important than others and looping allows the attorney conducting cross examination to highlight and repeat this important fact, so it is anchored in the minds of the jury. Loops emphasize certain facts or phrases.

The technique starts by asking a leading question to establish the fact you want to emphasis. You then use that desired fact in the body of the next question without re-asking the question. Finally, you connect the looped fact that contains the undisputed fact.

An example of the looping technique looks like this:

Q. You were convicted of robbery?
A. Yes

Q. Your robbery conviction was a felony?
A. Yes

Q. Your robbery conviction was that you stole construction equipment from your employer?
A. Yes

Q. After your robbery conviction you went to work for my client?
A. Yes

Q. When you went to work for my client you did not tell him you were convicted of robbery?
A. No

■ USE OF TRILOGIES

Another helpful technique during cross examination is the use of trilogies. As the name implies trilogies use three sets of facts or concepts that are related and linked together. They can be used to condition the jury to support your theory of the case while emphasizing important facts. Trilogies are found in great speeches and throughout literature. The use of just three words or terms are more memorable than other phasing. Three seems to be a magic number.

Creating trilogies is similar to the looping technique described above. You simply find a concept in your theory of the case, express it in three different ways and express them in three parts of leading questions.

Here is an example:

Q. You had a close and caring relationship with your brother?

Q. You went into business with your brother hoping you could work together and together build a profitable business?

Q. Your brother took the invention you made and filed for a patent in his name alone as the inventor?

Q. You felt betrayed by your brother?

Q. You felt neglected by your brother?

Q. You felt devastated by the way your brother treated you?

■ IMPEACHMENT BY PRIOR INCONSISTENT STATEMENT

One goal of cross examination is to impeach the witness by their prior inconsistent statement. Impeaching a witness by prior inconsistent statement means using a prior statement made by the witness that contradicts their current testimony to challenge their credibility. To impeach a witness in this manner, you first must identify the witness' prior statement. Review the witness's prior statements, such as statements made during a deposition, interview, or previous testimony, and identify any statements that contradict their current testimony. Once you have identified the prior statement obtain a copy of the prior statement, whether it's a transcript, recording, or written statement.

The current version of a fact or statement is normally established in direct examination or was established during cross examination or sometimes was volunteered. This witness will volunteer the new version because he thinks it is more favorable to his position and detrimental to the cross-examiner's case.

Next: you will need to either state or summarize the text to be impeached. This step is required to remind the fact finder of the testimony to be impeached. If you are going to state what the witness said on direct examination, you can either quote it verbatim or summarize the statement. If you quote verbatim you should have a copy of his direct testimony to avoid misquoting. If you summarize his statement, the witness will have to admit to making that statement. The key is to fairly summarize the witness's direct testimony as to the fact to be impeached.

You next need to introduce a phrase that sets up the impeachment that prepares the judge or jury that the statement they about to hear is inaccurate. You may ask the witness a question that sets the stage for the prior inconsistent statement like: As I understood your testimony on direct examination your latest thought is that when you signed the contract with Steve Snowden you signed under duress?

You were threatened by Mr. Snowden with physical violence if you did not sign the contract?

Once you confirmed the witness's testimony at trial you reveal the prior inconsistent statement and tie the witness to that statement by the following questions:

Q. You remember giving a deposition in this case on February 17, 2021?

Q. At that deposition, your attorney was present? Q. You were told that your testimony at your deposition can be used at trial?

Q. This is a copy of your deposition?

Q. Allow me to read from your deposition at page 47 line 3-10:

"When I signed the contract Mr. Snowden, and I had a friendly discussion and we both felt this contract would make both of us a lot of money?"

■ BE RESPECTFUL TO THE WITNESSES

It is important to remember that you don't want to badger a witness under cross examination. Jurors do not like it when you are attacking someone, unless they really believe that person is deserving of it. Rather than badgering, you want to use facts to discredit the witness. Also, recognize that there is a relationship between voir dire, where you first lay out the theory of the case to the jury, your opening statement, cross examination, and your closing argument. At trial, you have to keep your theory of the case in mind and all times. You want to keep bringing in your keywords and key phrases to imprint upon the jury your theory of the case and how the evidence you are presenting is consistent with the theory.

■ PRIMACY AND RECENCY

There is a psychological principle called primacy and it tells us that a fact finder is more likely to remember the first thing they hear for the longest period of time. That is why it's important to make a strong opening statement, filled with emotion and anchoring your tagline. There are certain things that you want the jurors to be repeating to themselves when they are doing their deliberations. The cross-examination of a key witness can be important in a trial. The key witness is typically someone who has first-hand knowledge of the events that led to the trial, and their testimony can be crucial in determining the outcome of the case. For this reason, the use of primacy of the questions and the evidence is important when you put your key witnesses on the witness stand.

The concept of primacy refers to the idea that the first information presented in a series or list is more likely to be remembered and given greater weight in decision-making than subsequent information. In psychology, the primacy effect is a cognitive bias that describes how people tend to remember and recall the first few items in a series better than the rest. This effect can occur when we learn new information or when we meet new people.

The primacy effect is thought to occur because the first items in a series receive more attention and are more deeply processed in memory than later items. This can lead to a stronger and more enduring memory trace for those items, which in turn can influence subsequent judgments and decisions. Understanding the primacy effect can be useful where the order in which information is presented can have a significant impact on how it is perceived and remembered.

The concept of recency refers to the idea that the most recent information presented in a series or list is more likely to be remembered and given greater weight in decision-making than earlier information. This effect is known as the recency effect. Similar to the primacy effect, the recency effect is a cognitive bias that describes how people tend to remember and recall the last few items in a series better than the rest.

The recency effect is thought to occur because the last items in a series are still fresh in our memory and have not been displaced by subsequent information. This can lead to a stronger and more immediate influence on judgments and decisions. The use of recency is effective during your closing argument. Primacy and recency are both important to start strong and end strong.

The recency effect can also be useful in a variety of contexts where the order in which information is presented can have a significant impact on how it is perceived and remembered. It is important to note, however, that the primacy and recency effects can sometimes compete with each other and that the context in which the information is presented can also play a role in which effect is stronger.

CHAPTER 26

THE RULE AGAINST HEARSAY

Probably the most heavily litigated concept in the law of evidence is the rule against hearsay. The rule against hearsay is a fundamental principle in the law of evidence that generally prohibits the admission of out-of-court statements made by someone other than the witness who is testifying, to prove the truth of the matter asserted in the statement.

In other words, if a person wants to offer a statement as evidence in court, and that statement was made by someone who is not present in court to testify, it may be excluded as hearsay, unless an exception applies. This is because such statements are considered unreliable, as the original speaker cannot be cross-examined, and may have been mistaken or dishonest when they made the statement.

The rule against hearsay is designed to ensure that the evidence presented in court is reliable, trustworthy, and subject to scrutiny and tested by the opposing party. There are, however, a number of exceptions to the rule against hearsay, which allow certain types of out-of- court statements to be admitted as evidence under certain circumstances.

In his tapes on the rules of evidence Irving Younger tells an amusing story explaining hearsay and one recognized exception. He describes a person who committed an armed robbery of a general store somewhere in Texas during the nineteenth century. The robber fled on foot. The store owner reported the theft to the local sheriff who came to the scene of the crime with a blood hound to track down the criminal. Within a short time, the blood hound was seen barking at the base of a large tree. Looking up from where the blood hound was barking there was an individual who had climbed up this tree a great distance.

At the trial on the charge of robbery, the defense attorney objected to evidence of the dog barking claiming the dog was essentially saying "that is the armed robber" and that statement would be hearsay because it was an out of court statement offered for the truth of the matter asserted. On appeal the appellate court in its infinite wisdom, disagreed. According to this appellate tribunal, the dog was not saying "that is the robber." What the dog was saying was "In my opinion that is the robber." Since the dog was an expert witness the dog's opinion was admissible as an exception to the hearsay rule.

Whether or not that was an actual case was not important because it taught a valuable lesson in understanding the concept of hearsay and a possible exception.

There are numerous exceptions to the rule against hearsay, and the specific exceptions may vary depending on the jurisdiction and the context of the case. However, some common exceptions to the rule against hearsay include:

Statements made by a party to the case: If a statement was made by a party to the case, it may be admissible as an admission against interest, as long as it was made voluntarily and is relevant to the case.

Dying declarations: Statements made by a person who believes they are about to die, and who has no hope of recovery, may be admissible as evidence in certain circumstances, particularly in cases of homicide.

Statements made for medical diagnosis or treatment: Statements made by a patient to a doctor or other medical professional for the purpose of medical diagnosis or treatment may be admissible as an exception to the hearsay rule.

Business records: Records made in the course of a business or organization may be admissible as an exception to the hearsay rule, provided that the records were made in the ordinary course of business and were kept as a matter of routine.

Excited utterances: Statements made by a person under the influence of sudden and extreme emotions or excitement may be admissible as an exception to the hearsay rule, as they are considered to be reliable because they were made spontaneously and without the opportunity for the person to reflect or fabricate.

Prior inconsistent statements: Statements made by a witness that are inconsistent with their testimony at trial may be admissible as an exception to the hearsay rule, to impeach the witness's credibility.

Statements against interest: Statements made by a person that are contrary to their own interests may be admissible as an exception to the hearsay rule, as they are considered to be more reliable than self-serving statements.

It's important to note that these exceptions are not exhaustive and other exceptions may exist depending on the jurisdiction and specific circumstances of the case. It is vitally important you be familiar with the rules of evidence including the hearsay rule and its exception before the trial. This can be the area of a motion in limine to get an advanced ruling.

CHAPTER 27

CLOSING ARGUMENT

By the time you get to the closing argument, the jurors have usually made up their minds about the case. They've heard all the evidence, they understand the tag line, and they've witnessed the direct and cross examination. The closing argument is when you get a chance to review the evidence in front of the jury.

This is when you go over the special verdict form with the jurors. I like to take the actual jury verdict form and go through each question, answering the questions for the jury based on the evidence that was presented at the trial.

Give them your reason for answering the questions in a way that will result in a verdict in favor of your client. You are recapping the evidence in a non-argumentative way, stating the facts, and pointing to all the evidence that proves your case.

A strong closing argument in a trial is crucial as it can be the last chance to persuade the jury or judge to rule in your favor. Your closing argument should be organized and structured. Begin with a clear statement of the case, summarize the evidence, and then present your main arguments in a logical sequence. Confidence is key when making a closing argument. Speak clearly, with conviction and sincerity, and maintain eye contact with the jury or judge.

Use emotional appeals: Emotional appeals can be effective in a closing argument.

Use examples and anecdotes to help the jury or judge connect emotionally with your argument.

Anticipate and rebut the opposing side's arguments. Address any weaknesses in your case and explain why they are not significant.

Use visual aids: Visual aids can be helpful in reinforcing your argument. Charts, graphs, and timelines can make your argument more compelling and memorable.

End your closing argument with a strong call to action, asking the jury or judge to rule in your favor. Make it clear what you want them to do and why.

Finally, practice your closing argument until you are comfortable with it. Practice in front of a mirror, a friend, or a colleague, and seek feedback to improve your delivery.

Remember, a strong closing argument is your last chance to persuade the jury or judge to rule in your favor, so make it count.

CHAPTER 28

TRIAL MOTIONS: PRE- AND POST- VERDICT

Federal courts require the parties to submit what is called "findings of facts and conclusions of law." The purpose of requiring findings of fact and conclusions of law in federal court is to provide a clear and well-reasoned basis for the court's decision. These findings and conclusions help to ensure that the court has considered all of the relevant evidence and legal arguments in the case, and that its decision is based on a sound legal and factual analysis.

Findings of fact are the court's determination of the relevant facts in the case, based on the evidence presented. These findings must be based on the evidence presented at trial or in other proceedings and must be supported by the record. The court must make findings of fact in order to decide in the case, as the law requires that the court's decision be based on the facts presented.

The conclusions of law, on the other hand, are the court's

application of the law to the facts of the case. These conclusions must be based on the relevant legal principles and precedent and must be supported by the court's reasoning. Conclusions of law are essential to the court's decision-making process, as they determine how the law applies to the facts of the case.

Together, the findings of fact and conclusions of law provide a clear and well-reasoned basis for the court's decision, which helps to ensure that the decision is fair, impartial, and based on the law and the facts of the case.

After the jury renders its verdict in federal court there are several available motions. It is important to be familiar with the available motions and the procedures to follow to preserve any issues your client may want to raise on appeal. Some of these motions need to be made after the case was submitted to the jury but before the jury rendered its verdict and others that need to be made within 28 days after the verdict was entered.

■ FEDERAL RULE 50

Federal Rule 50 is a rule of civil procedure that provides for a judgment as a matter of law (JMOL) in favor of a party in a case, either at the close of the plaintiff's case, the close of all the evidence, or after the jury has returned a verdict. The basis for Rule 50 is to allow a party to challenge the sufficiency of the evidence presented by the opposing party, and to request that the court enter a judgment in their favor as a matter of law.

The purpose of Rule 50 is to avoid unnecessary trials and to promote the efficient resolution of cases by allowing a court to take control of the case if it determines that the evidence is insufficient to support a verdict in favor of one party. This rule is based on the idea that parties should not be required to go through a trial if there is no genuine dispute of material fact and one party is entitled to a judgment as a matter of law.

To succeed on a motion for judgment as a matter of law, the moving party must show that there is no reasonable basis for a jury to find in favor of the non- moving party, based on the evidence presented. The court must view the evidence in the light most favorable to the non-moving party and must draw all reasonable inferences in their favor.

The basis for Rule 50 is to provide a mechanism for parties to seek judgment in their favor as a matter of law, based on the evidence presented, in order to promote the efficient resolution of cases and avoid unnecessary trials.

■ FEDERAL RULE 59

Federal Rule 59 governs the procedure for a motion for a new trial, alteration of a judgment, or amendment to the judgment in civil cases in the United States federal courts. The function of Rule 59 is to provide parties with a mechanism to challenge a jury verdict or a court's ruling after trial, and to give the court an opportunity to correct errors or omissions in its judgment or order.

The primary function of a motion for a new trial under Rule 59 is to seek a new trial on the basis of errors that occurred during the trial that may have affected the outcome. This could include errors in the admission or exclusion of evidence, improper jury instructions, or misconduct by the opposing party or the court. The party making the motion must show that the errors were substantial enough to have affected the verdict.

A motion to alter or amend the judgment under Rule 59(e) is similar to a motion for a new trial but is focused on errors or omissions in the court's final judgment or order. For example, a party may argue that the court made a mistake in applying the law or in calculating damages, and that the judgment should be corrected accordingly.

The function of Rule 59 is to ensure that parties are given a fair opportunity to challenge a judgment or verdict, and to provide the court with a mechanism to correct errors or omissions in its rulings.

■ FEDERAL RULE 60

Federal Rule 60 is a rule of civil procedure that governs the procedure for relief from a final judgment or order in civil cases in the United States federal courts. The purpose of Rule 60 is to provide parties with a mechanism to seek relief from a final judgment or order in certain limited circumstances.

The main purpose of Rule 60 is to provide a mechanism for a party to seek relief from a final judgment or order in situations where the judgment or order was entered as a result of mistake, inadvertence, surprise, excusable neglect, fraud, or other exceptional circumstances. The rule also provides for relief in situations where the judgment or order is void or has been satisfied, released, or discharged.

Rule 60 allows a party to seek relief from a final judgment or order through a motion filed with the court. The motion must be filed within a certain time period, depending on the basis for the motion. For example, a motion based on mistake, inadvertence, surprise, or excusable neglect must be filed within one year of the entry of the judgment or order, while a motion based on fraud or other exceptional circumstances must be filed within a reasonable time.

The purpose of Rule 60 is to provide parties with a limited opportunity to seek relief from a final judgment or order in certain circumstances, in order to ensure that justice is done, and that the outcome of the case is fair and equitable. However, the rule is not intended to provide a mechanism for a party to relitigate a case or to avoid the consequences of a strategic decision made during the course of the litigation.

■ FEDERAL RULE 62

Federal Rule 62 is a rule of civil procedure that governs the stay, enforcement, and relief from judgment or order in civil cases in the United States federal courts. The purpose of Rule 62 is to provide parties with a mechanism to seek relief from the enforcement of a judgment or order, to stay the enforcement of a judgment or order, or to provide security in order to obtain relief from the judgment or order.

The primary purpose of Rule 62 is to provide parties with a mechanism to seek a stay of the enforcement of a judgment or order pending appeal. The rule allows a party to seek a stay of the enforcement of a judgment or order by posting a bond or other security to ensure payment of the judgment or order if the appeal is unsuccessful.

In addition, Rule 62 also provides for relief from the enforcement of a judgment or order, such as a temporary restraining order or a preliminary injunction, if the party seeking relief can show that the judgment or order is unjust or that it would result in irreparable harm if it were enforced.

The purpose of Rule 62 is to provide parties with a mechanism to seek relief from the enforcement of a judgment or order, to stay the enforcement of a judgment or order pending appeal, or to provide for security in order to obtain relief from the judgment or order. This rule is intended to promote fairness and equity in the enforcement of judgments and orders, and to ensure that parties are not unfairly burdened by an unjust or incorrect judgment or order.

■ FEDERAL RULE 65

Federal Rule 65 is a rule of civil procedure that governs the issuance of temporary restraining orders and preliminary injunctions in civil cases in the United States federal courts. The purpose of Rule 65 is to provide parties with a mechanism to seek immediate relief from irreparable harm pending the resolution of the underlying case.

The main purpose of Rule 65 is to provide a mechanism for a party to seek a temporary restraining order or preliminary injunction in order to prevent irreparable harm or to maintain the status quo pending the resolution of the underlying case. A temporary restraining order is an emergency order that can be issued without notice to the opposing party and is intended to maintain the status quo until a hearing can be held to determine whether a preliminary injunction should be issued. A preliminary injunction is a court order that prohibits a party from taking certain actions, or requires a party to take certain actions, pending the resolution of the underlying case.

Rule 65 also provides for notice and a hearing before a preliminary injunction is issued, in order to ensure that both parties have an opportunity to be heard on the issue. The rule requires that the party seeking the injunction provide a bond or other security to ensure that the opposing party is not unfairly burdened by the injunction.

The purpose of Rule 65 is to provide parties with a mechanism to seek immediate relief from irreparable harm pending the resolution of the underlying case, while ensuring that both parties have an opportunity to be heard and that the opposing party is not unfairly burdened by the injunction. This rule is intended to promote fairness and equity in the resolution of civil cases in the federal courts.

CHAPTER 29

THE APPEAL

O nce upon a time, there was a man named Edgar who had been accused of a serious crime. He had been brought to trial, and despite his protests of innocence, the jury had found him guilty. Edgar was devastated. He knew that he had not committed the crime, but he had no way to prove it.

Edgar's lawyer was convinced that there had been a mistake made during the trial. He believed the judge gave an inappropriate jury instruction, precluded several witnesses when he granted a motion in limine, and allowed evidence to be improperly admitted over his objection. Because of these errors he believed that crucial evidence had been overlooked, and that Edgar had not been given a fair hearing. So, he decided to file an appeal.

The appeal was heard in a higher court, and Edgar's lawyer presented his case. He argued that certain evidence had not been considered, and that Edgar's rights had been violated in some way during the trial. The judge listened carefully to the arguments, and eventually agreed that there had been an error made during the trial.

As a result, the judge overturned the original verdict, and ordered a new trial to be held. Edgar was overjoyed. Finally, he had a chance to clear his name and prove his innocence.

The new trial was held, and this time, the evidence that had been overlooked during the first trial was presented. It was clear that Edgar had not committed the crime he had been accused of, and the jury quickly reached a verdict of not guilty.

Edgar was exonerated, and he felt a tremendous sense of relief and gratitude. He knew that he would never have been able to clear his name without the help of his lawyer, who had worked tirelessly on his behalf. Thanks to the appeal, justice had been served, and Edgar was able to move on with his life, free from the shadow of the false accusations that had been hanging over him. Law is a serious business. The courts have the power to take away your liberty in a criminal trial or take away all your property in a civil trial. The cases that do not settle or get dismissed before trial are cases where there is a dispute over some facts. Anybody who has been a defendant in a criminal trial facing a long prison term, or being sued for their life savings and facing a punitive damage claim are likely experiencing high levels of stress because the outcomes are uncertain. Anything can happen.

It is imperative when you are representing a party to a lawsuit to make sure you create a sufficient record in the trial court in case you need to file an appeal. Despite your efforts there is always the possibility an error occurred that you want to raise on appeal.

■ PRESERVE THE RECORD FOR AN APPEAL

Preserving a record in the trial court for an appeal is essential to ensure that the appellate court has all the necessary information and evidence to review the lower court's decision. Here are some ways to preserve a record in the trial court for an appeal:

Make timely objections: During the trial, if an attorney believes that the opposing party's evidence is inadmissible or that there has been a mistake made, they should make a timely objection on the record. This will ensure that the objection is preserved for the appeal.

Make timely motions: If an attorney believes that the trial court has made an error, they can make a motion asking the court to correct the error. This should be done in a timely manner and on the record so that it is preserved for the appeal.

Record the trial proceedings: The trial proceedings should be recorded, either by a court reporter or by electronic means. This record will serve as the basis for the appellate court's review of the case.

File written motions and objections: In addition to making oral objections and motions, attorneys should also file written motions and objections with the court. This will ensure that the objections and motions are clearly documented for the appeal.

Ensure that the record is complete: Before the appeal is filed, attorneys should review the record to ensure that it is complete and accurate. This includes reviewing the trial transcript, exhibits, and any other documents or recordings related to the case. The procedure to perfect an appeal may vary depending on the jurisdiction and the court involved. However, in general, the following are the basic steps involved in perfecting an appeal:

■ PERFECTING AN APPEAL

The first step in perfecting an appeal is to file a notice of appeal with the appropriate court. This notice must be filed within a specific time frame, which varies depending on the jurisdiction and the type of case involved. Once the notice of appeal is filed, the appellant must order a transcript of the trial proceedings from the court reporter. This transcript will be necessary for the appeal.

After the transcript is prepared, the record on appeal must be filed with the appellate court. This record includes the transcript, any exhibits admitted as evidence, and any other documents related to the trial.

The parties must file briefs outlining their arguments and legal authorities. The appellant must file an opening brief, which the appellee can respond to with an answering brief. The appellant may also file a reply brief. The parties may also have the opportunity to present oral arguments before the appellate court. During this argument, the attorneys for each side can present their case and answer questions from the judges. After reviewing the record, briefs, and any oral arguments, the appellate court will issue a decision. This decision may affirm, reverse, or modify the lower court's decision, or it may remand the case back to the lower court for further proceedings.

ENDNOTES

1. Chris Voss *Never Split the Difference*
2. Tieger, *A Summary of Recently Conducted Behavioral Research;* Levine *Jury Selection* (2004) section 4:34
3. see Moore *Trial by Schema: Cognitive Filters;* Levine *On Trial Advocacy* (2004) chapter 4.8
4. Levine *On Trial Advocacy; Jury Selection*
5. Moore *Trial by Schema*
6. Tieger, *A Summary of Recently Conducted Behavioral Research;* Levine *Jury Selection* (2004) section 4:34
7. J. Gilbert & W. Johnson, *National Jury Product;* Vinson on *What Makes Jurors Tick?*
8. Irving Younger on *Trial Advocacy.*

ABOUT THE AUTHOR

Robert G. Klein is an experienced business litigation trial attorney in Los Angeles, California who handles a multitude of litigation cases throughout the state of California with an emphasis on intellectual property litigation.

He earned a Bachelor of Science Degree in psychology before attending the business school at DePaul University where he studied business and accounting. He obtained a CPA certificate and obtained a Juris Doctorate degree in law. Klein is also a member of the American Society of Trial Consultants. And he appeared for oral argument before the United States Supreme Court on a 14th Amendment due process case involving government contracting.

As a prestigious trial lawyer who understands the importance and nuances of jury selection, Klein has represented clients in the critical areas of intellectual property issues, copyright infringement business and trademark issues. Klein continues to tackle difficult cases and is determined to achieve the best results for his clients. In his writing, Klein sheds light on complicated subjects found in modern law today.

Known for going above and beyond for his clients, Klein's love and respect for the law is clear. As a lifelong student of the law, he doesn't rest on his laurels.

Robert is the author of an additional book, *Counterfeiter*, which tells a fascinating story in novelized form that takes you through the fundamentals of trademark law. Available on Amazon and other online retailers.

For more information and to contact Robert, visit
www.kleinonlitigation.com